AGING OUT

A true story about
the pitfalls and promise
of life after foster care

Alton Carter

THE ROADRUNNER PRESS

Published by The RoadRunner Press
Oklahoma City, Oklahoma
www.TheRoadRunnerPress.com

© 2016 by Alton Carter
Cover Illustration © 2016 Tim Jessell
Cover Copyright © 2016 The RoadRunner Press
All rights reserved.

Cover design by Tim Jessell

The RoadRunner Press is committed to publishing works of quality
and integrity. The story, the experiences, and the words shared here
are the author's alone. Some names have been changed
out of respect for those who lived this story.

Printed in the USA

Library of Congress LCCN: 2016949020

Publisher's Cataloging-In-Publication Data
(Prepared by The Donohue Group, Inc.)
Names: Carter, Alton.
Title: Aging out : a true story about the pitfalls and promise of life
after foster care / Alton Carter.
Description: Oklahoma City, Oklahoma : The RoadRunner Press, [2016] |
Interest age level: 16 and up.
Identifiers: LCCN 2016949020 | ISBN 978-1-937054-28-1 (hardcover) |
ISBN 978-1-937054-29-8 (trade paper) | ISBN 978-1-937054-31-1 (ebook)
Subjects: LCSH: Carter, Alton. | Foster children--United States--Social
conditions. | African American youth--Social conditions.
Classification: LCC HV881 .C37 2016 (print) | LCC HV881 (ebook) |
DDC 362.73/30973--dc23

For my church family—
thank you for believing in me

"A failure is not always a mistake.
It may simply be the best one can
do under the circumstances.
The real mistake is to stop trying."

— B. F. Skinner
American author
(1904–1990)

Introduction

My departure from an abusive home at the age of nine and what came after were tragic, but I must admit my departure from high school and aging out of foster care came with a whole new, unexpected bag of problems. Being the first in my family to stay in school past ninth grade, the first to graduate from high school, and the first to win a college scholarship was a dream come true for me, but I realize now it came with no guarantee that I would do well in college or life going forward.

I didn't know that at age seventeen. I thought breaking our family's dropout cycle would give me the confidence to let go of my past, to put down the bricks I carried, and to thrive on my own. But one of the little dark secrets that no one shares with teens is how quickly life gets real after high school—no matter who you are.

There's a reason the six-year college graduation rate in this country hovers at about 53 percent. Yes, I said six years; most students no longer finish in four, and for former foster kids, the graduation rate plunges to 4 percent, and it takes even those until age twenty-six to get that diploma.

And those are the lucky ones. According to Covenant House, which provides services and shelter to at-risk youths across the country, more than twenty thousand young people age out of the U.S. foster care system every single year—most are only eighteen years old and lack the life skills necessary to live on their own. Of those, nearly 40 percent become homeless.

Looking back, I realize now my seventeen-year-old self was neither prepared nor ready for what was about to come his way—and he spent way too much time dwelling on the past and how life and people had wronged him and not enough on how to cope. To say that I made mistakes after high school would be an understatement. To say I hurt others, even those trying to help me, is sadly true. Truth be told, for the next fifteen years, I felt as if I was shooting in the dark when it came to the game of life. I had no idea how to be a friend or a boyfriend, much less a good student or a responsible adult, an employee or a husband or father.

Yet whenever it seemed I had no one to turn to and nowhere to go, the voices of those who had loved and stood by me in the past would return and remind me of who I was and what I was capable of being. The memories of those people, combined with the new caring folks in my life, would ultimately be what helped me overcome the demons from my past.

I'm not saying it was easy. I'm not saying there weren't a lot of lonely, sleepless, and scary nights—many of them spent on a stranger's couch. And those were the good nights. Still, I found if I just kept putting one foot in front of the other, if I didn't give up, if I held on for one more day . . . and if I took the help that presented itself, my life slowly improved. My only regret is those years didn't have to be as difficult as society made them for me or as I made them for myself.

I was just a kid with so many questions that I needed answered; unfortunately, I did not have it in me to ask the very people who had the information that I wanted and needed. Maybe I was afraid of what they would say. Maybe I didn't even know what I didn't know. Very possibly, I didn't know whom to even ask. But knowing what I know now, I can't help but believe that had there only been more counselors along the way to detect academic shortfalls and learning disabilities in kids like me earlier in school, had there only been more case workers along the way to prepare kids like me for leaving high school and aging out, had there only been college advisers who knew the baggage kids like me bring to college, that my experience at college might have been better . . . and surely so would the lives of so many other young people, foster kids or not.

I always say my story is no better or worse than anyone else's—we all have bricks that we carry. I share mine here because I know there are many others out there who need to know that they are not alone, who need to know people will appear in their life who want to help . . . and it is okay to let them.

In the end, this story is about the ugly truth of what happened to me after aging out of the foster care system. It is a bittersweet tale, and I hope it will remind all who read it that everyone deserves a second chance and that you can never know what others are dealing with, so much can be hidden behind a smile.

—Alton Carter

Chapter 1

A Catch-22

I never got used to waking up in a house that was not my own. I would open my eyes, blink, and slowly realize I was in a bed and not on the hard floor of my grandma's house squeezed between the warm bodies of my siblings and cousins. Almost eight years gone, and that morning reality always made the knot in my stomach tighten.

People forget how ingrained the routines of family become and what comfort they give, especially to children. It can take years for a new place to feel like home, and I changed addresses every year or so in the beginning, after walking away from home at age nine.

The longest I ever stayed anywhere was the Oklahoma Lions Boys Ranch in Perkins, Oklahoma, and my last foster home—about three years at each. My final high school years I lived in a big house in Cushing, Oklahoma, with a nice couple named Marcy and Phil.

Marcy and Phil fed me well, gave me a safe place to stay, and even went to some of my football games and my high school graduation. I repaid them by resenting the time they spent with their own children and being jealous that they weren't my own family. And no, the contradiction never occurred to me at the time.

The only thing I wanted was to belong.

To somebody.

Several times during my time with them, Marcy and Phil introduced me as their son, and it made me feel so good. I used to think if they could only have told me a thousand times that they loved me, maybe I would have felt more like a son than a foster kid.

In reality, I knew lots of parents, especially fathers, who never told their own kids "I love you," and deep down I think I knew that Marcy and Phil would never be my real parents anyway. They were stand-ins. Good people, paid by the state, to put a roof over my head. And I'd heard about or experienced enough horror stories to know to be grateful for them. Still, I wish there had been a way they could have made me feel more like their son during the time I spent with them.

I always felt like a misfit in the foster homes where I lived, and that was made worse when foster parents would bad-mouth my mom. Even as a little boy, I knew foster parents should never speak ill of a foster child's biological parents or family—those are slurs that hurt more than slaps, and they can never be taken back.

I had foster parents tell me:

"Your mother is the worst mother in the world."

"Your family members are all worthless bums."

"Your mom doesn't care about you or your brothers and sisters or she would have made better choices."

I heard foster parents call my mom all sorts of bad and profane names. Their words opened wounds in me that would take decades to heal.

By definition, I knew I was a "foster kid," but I hated the term because to me, it implied that I was temporary. It was just another reminder that I was not a part of this family or that family or any family that counted, for that matter, and that someone else was taking care of me because my real family could not.

The irony, of course, is that if any of my foster parents had ever tried to call me son, I might well have rejected them. Still, that didn't mean I didn't want one of them to say it. Such is the catch-22 of being a foster child.

What most people don't realize is you can live with foster parents in their home, eat at their table, wash in their tub, and still be all but invisible to them. And for someone like me, who wanted nothing more than to be seen and to belong, it made for an intolerable existence.

I don't recall any foster parents ever asking me about my life before I came to live with them, what I wanted to be when I grew up, what my fears were, what my dreams were. Yes, we talked about things sometimes, but I don't recall any of those conversations ever getting past what was in my case file or what they'd been told by my caseworker. Unprompted, I would occasionally try to tell one of them a little about me or what would make me feel more comfortable in their home, but such confidences always fell on deaf ears.

It wasn't like any of them tried to tell me much either. I don't recall anyone ever sitting me down and telling me anything of importance, like why it's important to study and do your best at school (it helps with college entrance, with college preparedness, and with figuring out what you're good at so you can pick a major and then a career some day). No one told me about registering to vote or signing up for selective service or how to get a checking account, much less the importance of having a savings account for emergencies or getting regular physicals, particularly for someone like me who is borderline diabetic.

Being unaware allowed me to enjoy life one day at a time. Clueless, I spent most of my time fretting over the past, never realizing that by looking back instead of forward, I was narrowing what my future could be, what job I might someday get, what life I could someday have.

The only lecture I ever heard my Cushing foster dad give wasn't even initially to me; I just happened to overhear the beginning of it. I was upstairs in my room, and downstairs Phil started yelling at one of the other foster boys about what was going to happen to him if he didn't start making better choices.

Phil rarely yelled at anyone, so I knew he was upset. After saying that underage drinking in his house was not an option, Phil summoned the rest of us who were home downstairs to the living room.

I took a seat by the fireplace, and the other two boys settled on the couch. Once we were all seated, Phil got right in front of us so he could see all of our faces.

"I want you all to listen up," he said. "Right now, you are minors and wards of the state, and the courts are limited to what sort of punishment they can give you when you break the law. Because you are a minor, you are more likely to get a slap on the wrist when you break the law."

He paused to make sure he had our attention.

"There will come a day when you will turn eighteen, and your DHS worker will no longer be able to get you out of trouble. You will have to sit in jail and answer for what you've done."

He told us that most people think foster kids are in foster care not because they are escaping a troubled home but because they themselves made bad choices, got into trouble, and were finally taken away because their parents couldn't control them.

"Lots of people will feel sorry for you while you're a foster child, but when you turn eighteen and break the law, neither the police nor the judge will give a damn that you were a foster kid once," he said.

"If your childhood is mentioned at all," Phil added, "it will be to prove to the rest of the world that you were a bad kid then and now you're an adult who doesn't care about the law."

With that, Phil turned and walked off.

For a few minutes, the other foster kids and I sat there speechless, and then one by one, we went our separate ways.

Later that night in my room, I wondered if that was what parenting looked like. I had never thought about being an adult, much less about how it might differ from being a kid. I had watched the adults in my life abuse alcohol on a daily basis; I had had uncles who forced my siblings and me to drink whiskey when we were barely in grade school. I couldn't remember anyone in my family ever warning me away from using drugs or from breaking the law, much less telling me that such actions could land me in jail once I turned eighteen.

Phil must care about me to take the time to say those things to me, I thought. It was a new feeling, and I went to bed happy to have Phil in my life, even if it was only for a short time. Still, in the days to come, I did what I could to hide how I admired Phil. Keeping people at arm's length was how I made sure no one could ever hurt me.

It never occurred to me that had I showed Phil how I felt that it might have brought us closer and might have been the start of the loving relationship for which I was so hungry.

Chapter 2

College Prep

As my senior year got under way, talk amongst my classmates turned to turning eighteen, moving out, and going to college. Most of my friends planned to go to college in the fall, but tired of their parents' rules, they were all ready to move out of their house as soon as they could. I joined in their conversations about moving away or getting an apartment, but secretly, I was afraid of turning eighteen and having to take care of myself. In front of my friends, I pretended I was ready for college, even though I wasn't. And I never shared with any of them the fact that, being a foster kid, turning eighteen would trigger changes in my life I would not be able to control.

By October, everyone was taking the ACT (some for a second or third time), filling out applications for schools, and choosing college roommates. Since neither my foster parents nor anyone in my family had ever attended college, I was clueless about what was involved. If my high school counselor hadn't told me that I needed to sign up to take the ACT, I might never have done so in time.

In December 1997, the school counselor arranged for a group of us to go to Stillwater, Oklahoma, where my family lived, to take the test at Oklahoma State University. By then, many of my friends had taken the ACT multiple times in an effort to raise their scores. Several of us rode together that day, and I remember hearing the other kids mumbling about "I got a nineteen" and "My best was a twenty-three." I had no idea what they were talking about.

The closer we got to campus, the more scared I became. I had never been good at taking tests, and while everyone else seemed to have already completed prep tests or courses to prepare for the day's exam, I knew I hadn't. I wasn't prepared, but I had made the trip. I decided I would take the ACT and hope I got lucky and scored high enough not to embarrass myself.

We filed into the testing room, and I took a seat at a desk on which I found two No. 2 pencils and an exam booklet. The room was hushed. A woman walked to the front and began giving us the instructions we were to follow. Before she could finish, I was so overwhelmed my hands were shaking, and I was having trouble holding my pencil. The test began, and with the first question, I knew I was out of my element. Time passed, and I could hear people turning pages, while I still had quite a few blanks to fill on page one.

The ACT exam that day was the longest, most frightening academic event I have ever experienced. Because I was not a good reader, I did not comprehend most of the test questions, especially in the reading and grammar section. Being not particularly good at math, I guessed on the majority of the math problems. Unable to remember dates and facts, I staggered through the history section.

My only relief came in the section on science. At least there I felt I answered more questions than I guessed on.

On the ride to OSU, someone had asked what you should do if you didn't know the answer to a question on the ACT.

"If you don't know an answer," one of the guys said, "pick 'C' on the Scantron; you'll have a better chance of getting it right."

His advice had stuck with me, and so every time I came to a question that I didn't understand or couldn't answer (which was more often than not), I filled in the box for "C." When I finished, my answer sheet had so many "Cs" it looked more like wallpaper than part of an exam.

On the way home, my friends talked about how they thought they had done and speculated on what scores they might get.

I sat in the back seat, silent.

I knew I had not done well on the test, and I believed when my scores came back, they would confirm exactly what I already knew about myself: I was dumb and not smart enough to go to college.

A few weeks later, I came home to find Marcy waiting for me.

"Alton, you have some mail from OSU," she said. "I put it on the counter in the kitchen."

I'll never forget how my stomach turned over at her words; feeling as if I was about to throw up, I ran in the kitchen, grabbed the letter, and ran up to my room. I sat on my bed and stared at the envelope for what felt like hours.

When I finally found the courage to open it, I shuddered: my ACT score was an eleven.

It was not that I was surprised at having done poorly; I knew the exam had not gone well. But I had never heard of anyone getting an eleven. Most of my friends had gotten at least a twenty.

I tore the letter up and threw it in the trash.

In the days and years to come, when anyone asked me how I had done on the ACT, I always said that I'd gotten a seventeen. It was a lie. But I didn't care. I couldn't let people know how stupid I was.

Chapter 3

Graduation

I had been okay with living in the small rural town of Cushing where everybody knows everybody, but nothing about somebody like me. It was enough to be living with someone who fed me and did not beat or abuse me.

Most teens just want to find a crowd and fit in, blend in so other teens won't single them out for taunts or scorn. I think, like love, I wanted that even more as a foster kid.

The very nature of being a foster kid makes it easy to overhear something or experience something that leaves you with the impression that being a foster kid is a bad thing. It's not. We're survivors. We've survived what many people couldn't dream of enduring. We should take pride in that, and I think if more foster parents and teachers and other adults took the time to point that out to foster kids and the rest of the world, the stigma of being a foster child could go the way of the dodo bird.

Unfortunately, that was not the case back in my high school days, at least not for me. I always felt branded with a big "F" as in "the Foster Kid." Now the irony of this is, when my first book, *The*

Boy Who Carried Bricks, came out in 2015, quite a few former friends and classmates from Cushing told me they had not known I was in foster care back in high school, much less that I came from a troubled family that lived in another town.

It was a good reminder for me.

Everyone has problems, and most of us don't have enough time to solve our own, much less worry about the problems of others. Because I didn't realize that in my Cushing days, however, my high school graduation day dawned with all the promise of a historic day, which it was, but ended with me in a funk. By graduating from high school, I had officially done something no one else in my family had ever done, but the ceremony was bittersweet. Afterward, everyone seemed to have boatloads of relatives wishing them well and snapping photos—everyone, that is, but me. I had no one.

My mother didn't show, nor did any of my siblings or cousins make the twenty-five-minute drive. It was what I had expected, but it still hurt. Not that I would let anyone know that. It also seemed to make me, the foster kid without a family, more conspicuous than ever, at least in my mind. I tried to hide my embarrassment by taking as many pictures with other people as I could.

In the middle of taking just such a snapshot, I saw my grandparents walking up to the crowd. They had missed my graduation ceremony but showed up in time for a few Kodak moments. I knew everyone else had noticed their late arrival, but the last thing I wanted was for anyone to feel sorry for me or try to say something to cheer me up. Instead, I went to my grandparents, took a few pictures with them, and then convinced them to leave as soon as possible.

They insisted on taking me back to my foster home and even came in to visit for a while. Before heading back to Stillwater, they also both took the time to have a few words with me.

"I'm proud of you, Alton," Grandpa Carter said.

"We're glad you stayed in Cushing and finished school," said Grandma Carter. "I'm proud of you."

If only I had been open to what they were saying. Instead, still miffed about their being late, I said a fast good-bye, went to my room, shut the door, and flopped on the bed, where I proceeded to spend the night feeling sorry for myself, hating the past, worrying about the future, and wondering what I would do next—while all over Cushing my fellow classmates celebrated our special day with family and then with each other well into the night.

Chapter 4

My Last Summer

Foster kids age out of the foster care system at eighteen, but in a way, all kids age out then. Some teens turn eighteen and are promptly shown the door by their parents. Others turn eighteen and run for the door, away from abusive fathers, away from a mother's rules, away from however life has so far disappointed them. And then there are the teens who turn eighteen and run full tilt toward college and their future.

The difference is that even the kid who is pushed out the door has a stable home to which he can return or visit at holidays, and the same can rarely be said for the teen who ages out of foster care.

Usually, turning eighteen coincides with senior year or graduating from high school, but not for me. Younger than most of my classmates, I would not turn eighteen until the next September, so in a way I got a reprieve.

I got to stay with Phil and Marcy through the summer.

Looking back, I burned through that last summer in Cushing like cheap oil. I can't believe I did so little. I stayed away from Stillwater, except for a few trips to play basketball at the university sports annex, so I could avoid seeing my family. I was afraid of what they would say to me. I worked a little with Phil in his upholstery shop to earn a little cash, and I hauled hay with some friends once a week or so for the same reason.

I spent the rest of my time in bed. I was scared and alone and had no idea what was going to happen to me. Every tick of the clock just brought me closer to being all on my own, with no safety net. I realize now I was probably suffering from depression by then.

My best memories of that summer are working with Jeff and Tim, two brothers I knew from Cushing High School who owned their own hay-hauling business. They'd heard I had hauled hay back in my days at the boys ranch outside nearby Perkins, Oklahoma, and asked if I might like to work for them.

"Sure, I could use the work," I said.

"Great, we'll pick you up tonight," one of the brothers said.

"I've never hauled hay at night," I said, a little uneasily. "Why would we do it in the dark?"

Tim explained that they'd been hauling hay since they were little boys, and an Oklahoma summer was too hot during the day to work in the fields.

"It's best to get the hay out at night," he said. "It's much cooler."

So that evening, the brothers showed up at the house driving a big ol' truck with a hay-bale loader attached. We headed to a pasture, where the older brother, Jeff, showed me the way they stacked hay bales. Once I got it, Jeff climbed in the cab to drive, while Tim and I crawled on the trailer. We started on the outside of the field, circling it, picking up bales as fast as we could manage. Once the trailer was four deep in hay bales, we left to unload our load.

It was a twenty-minute ride to deliver the hay, and we chatted as we drove. I told Tim that when I hauled hay in Perkins, we did it in the heat of the day, and work never stopped, no matter how hot it got.

"Our ranch dad had us in the fields from as soon as the sun came up, and we stayed there until dark," I said.

Tim laughed, and before I could take offense, he said, "Our dad had us do the same thing when he was running the business, but now that it's our business, we get to decide when we want to be in the field."

We both laughed at that, and as we fell silent, I thought about how their dad had made them do exactly what my ranch dad had. I was a bit embarrassed.

For years, I had told myself that no one had ever gone through what I went through on those miserable, hot days at the boys ranch, and yet here were two Cushing boys telling me they'd had to face the same heat as little boys in the hay field, just like me. At that moment, my hay-hauling days in Perkins didn't seem quite so bad.

We turned off the dirt road onto a long drive and made our way to a big barn. Jeff backed the trailer into the barn, parked the truck, and then he and Tim each took a place behind the trailer.

"You throw the bales to us," Tim instructed in a firm but not unkind voice, "and we'll stack 'em."

I nodded. One by one, I threw the bales off the truck to the brothers, who then piled them one by one against the wall of the barn. When the trailer was empty, we returned to the field and started the process all over again. We made round-trip after round-trip between field and barn until the sun peeked over the trees to the east.

Once it climbed above the trees, it was time to stop and head home. The brothers dropped me off after work at Phil and Marcy's.

"We'll pick you up tomorrow night, if you still want to work," one said.

"Sure, I'll see you then," I replied.

I walked into the house, took a shower, and crawled into bed. I slept until almost dinnertime, and when I went to get up, every muscle in my body cried out for me to stay put. Aching with pain, I made my way downstairs. I knew better than to sit back down, so I spent the next half hour trying to walk out the soreness in my muscles. My walking took me into Phil's shop.

"How'd the hay hauling go?" he asked.

"Fine, but my whole body hurts, and they're going to be back for me tonight."

Phil laughed, and then with a smile on his face, he looked up and said, "The good thing about pain is, as long as you're feeling pain, it's your body's way of letting you know you are still alive."

"I'm livin' it up, then," I said, with a grin.

I waddled out of the shop to get myself something to eat before the brothers showed up. They were counting on me, and so I needed to fight through the pain. I also made myself a vow that I would not complain that night, no matter how badly I hurt.

Chapter 5

The Gift of Work

Growing up, the only person I ever saw work a full-time job was my Grandpa Carter, so in my mind, most adults just didn't work.

I realize that someone who didn't grow up in a household like ours might find that hard to believe. After all, the whole world works. Moms and dads work. Aunts and uncles work. Little kids in small towns toss newspapers in the wee hours of the morning; city kids collect and recycle aluminum cans; grade-schoolers babysit. Even some grandparents work.

But while you see people working every single day of your life at school, at the grocery store, at the gas station, at the local fast-food joint—including your own foster parents, these people aren't your people. My people were sitting on the ratty couch in Grandma Carter's house or on a bunk in jail.

And they were the ones I looked to as far as what was possible for me.

Grandpa Carter was the anomaly. He not only worked, but he worked two jobs—days at OSU maintenance, nights as a baseball referee. He was devoted to both, and even as a boy, I could tell he took pride in his work. His employees at OSU seemed to respect him; so did the other referees at the ball games. His coworkers loved him. I remember folks from work bringing him all sorts of gifts on his birthday and holidays. He was extremely good with people.

One day when I was about nine, I got to go to work with my grandpa. He had me sorting mail in his office when he suddenly turned and told me he had to step out for a few minutes.

"I'm leaving you in charge," he said.

Grandpa had no sooner disappeared around the corner than I was out on the floor telling everyone how my grandpa had left me in charge. I don't recall saying it meanly, nor was I trying to be bossy. I just wanted everyone to know that I was the boss until my grandpa got back.

A short time later, Grandpa returned, and called me into his office. "I was watching you try to be in charge while I was gone," he told me.

Seems he hadn't left but only stepped out of sight so he could watch me trying to run the place while he was gone. I could tell by the look on his face that I had disappointed him.

"Alton, if you want the respect of your employees, then you need to give them the same respect you want," Grandpa said. "A good boss leads by example, and he would never ask his employees to do something he wouldn't do."

I squirmed at his words. He caught and held my gaze. His face grew serious. "I heard you tell the other employees several times that you were the boss. Alton, if you have to tell people you're the boss, you're not in charge. A boss does not have to remind people over and over again that they answer to him. Everyone knows who the boss is by the way he conducts himself."

Grandpa taught me that day what it means to be a leader, but because he worked outside the home, I rarely saw how he led or went about doing his job. In fact, I probably learned the most about work from my ranch dad while living at the boys ranch in Perkins.

That man never accepted anything that was not our best effort, no matter the task. He also almost always had some advice on how the task could have been done better. He pushed us to be proud of whatever we did, whether it was hauling hay, cutting wood, or digging graves.

"You leave your name on every job you do, so it's important that you give each one your best," he once told me.

We worked long hours at the ranch, 365 days a year, taking care of the animals, cleaning stalls, doing household chores. In the beginning, I hated and resented every task. I realize now it was because I had never seen anyone work like we did there.

As time passed, I grew to appreciate some of what our ranch dad was trying to teach us, and I wanted him to be proud of me, as well as, the work that I did.

He was not a kind man, and he did not give pats on the back. Lucky for me, not getting in trouble for doing a terrible job was praise enough in those days. More than once, he bluntly reminded me that if I didn't work, I would find myself on welfare someday, just like the rest of my family.

His words cut. I had grown up watching adults not work. It's not a pretty sight, especially not at the end of the month when the adults on the couch start to get antsy because there's nothing left in the cupboards or the refrigerator and their disability or welfare check isn't due for another day. I have seen my relatives verbally assault the mailman when their check didn't arrive on the first day of the month.

Even as a little boy, I knew I did not want to grow up and be like that; if I was going to be like anyone, it was my grandpa.

My last few years of high school in Cushing, I worked some in my foster dad Phil's upholstery shop. He worked the extremely long hours and workweek of a small business owner, trying to make ends meet in a world that doesn't guarantee an entrepreneur a regular paycheck.

I noticed he paid attention to every little detail on every single job he took, making sure each piece of furniture he worked on was restored to the best of his ability.

I once asked him why he did what he did. I don't think he thought twice before answering.

"I love to see people's reaction when I've made something old of theirs look new again," he said.

Aging Out

I remember being surprised by his answer. I had thought he did it for the money, and yes, he did work to support his family. But to Phil, restoring furniture was about more than the cash it brought in. And I never forgot that.

Chapter 6

My Relationship with Money

My relationship with money was simple: I didn't have any.

In Cushing, none of the other foster boys had any either, nor did any of us have a part-time job, and I don't remember anyone ever suggesting that we should get one. I also don't remember any of us making the connection between being jobless and an empty wallet.

Man, we were so clueless.

As a senior, I kept busy with school and sports, and I had made a little money working now and then for Phil, all of which I put in a jar in my room. The jar never got very full because it doubled as my bank. If I needed or wanted anything, from a movie ticket to a candy bar, the money had to come out of my jar.

Not surprisingly, I made sure to eat either at home as much as possible or at school. When everyone else went off campus for lunch, 99 percent of the time I ate in the cafeteria. If I did happen to go with the others, I never ordered anything. The few times someone noticed and asked why, I told them I wasn't hungry; it was easier than saying I didn't have any money. You'd be surprised how rarely anyone asked.

Aging Out

I missed out on a lot of things during high school—church camps, school trips, class ring—because I had no money, and I didn't want to make things worse for my foster parents by asking for anything more. I told myself I didn't care, that I didn't want a class ring or anything else for that matter. Thank God for the high school booster club, which made sure kids had money for a snack when playing out-of-town football and basketball games.

After high school, not having a vehicle—or even a bicycle—also made it hard to get a summer job in our rural community, so I was grateful when Jeff and Tim let me work off and on with them hauling hay, especially since they didn't seem to mind having to pick me up and take me home each time. I remember one of the brothers telling me that their parents had made them pay for their own trucks, proof as to how working a steady job could pay off.

Since I only worked when the brothers needed extra help and could come and get me, I didn't work more than about once a week all summer. What money I earned, I think, I spent on clothes.

Here I was about to move away from the only stable home I'd known and in a matter of months age out of foster care and be all on my own—no one to pay my rent or buy me food. Yet it never occurred to me to save what I made for what was coming.

Because of my family, I knew welfare and food stamps were a possibility after I turned eighteen. However, I wanted to stand on my own two feet. To this very day, I've adhered to that.

Unfortunately, no one had yet to talk to me about money or checking accounts or credit cards or credit scores or even how loans work—much less how they all could be both a blessing and a curse. I had never thought about where to get money because my whole life, I'd had none.

That reality, coupled with the anxiety I was beginning to feel about moving out of Phil and Marcy's house, left me spending most of my summer days in bed. I played a little basketball, but mostly I stayed in the house in my room. This was not like a kid holing up in his room with a TV and video games or a record collection. I didn't have such things. No, this was just me, alone, with myself, in a room. I now realize I'd probably been falling into depression for some time.

And then I got a break. My grandpa called and offered to help me buy a car. He said he didn't have much money, but he would do what he could to help me find something to drive to college. I'd accepted a scholarship to play football at Southwestern College in Winfield, Kansas, about two hours from home, and I'd be leaving in late July for preseason training with the team. I immediately knew just the car.

One of my classmate's parents had bought him a new set of wheels, and he was selling his old car. I called him up and asked how much he wanted for it, and when he told me $500, I knew it would soon be mine.

Two days later, with Grandpa's $350 and the $150 I still had from hauling hay, I bought the car, a four-door sedan with peeling blue paint, dark gray seat covers, and a headliner that had pulled away from the roof in a few places. The car's motor mount was broken, so the motor shook when you started it. I didn't care, though; it was my first car, and I was proud of it.

Chapter 7

You Can't Go Home Again

There was just one problem with suddenly being the owner of a car: All I had was a driver's permit.

I had flunked the driving part of the driving exam, but neither Phil nor Marcy knew this. I had lied to them and told them I'd passed. I had then kept my little secret to myself, hoping no one would find out.

Unlike other teens, whose parents taught them how to drive—just like they had taught them how to ride a bike as children—and who encouraged their sons and daughters to practice in the pasture or parking lot before trying to pass a driver's test, I had just winged the exam, thinking I might never have need of a license anyway.

Grandpa's gift had changed all that.

And when you're someone who has never had anything, a little thing like a valid driver's license is not going to stop you from driving your new car.

The day after I bought the car, I told Phil that I wanted to go to Stillwater and visit my family for a few days before heading north to college.

"I don't think that's a good idea," he replied. He didn't say it, but I knew he thought my family would try to talk me out of going away to college. Although Phil was only looking out for me, I got upset and accused him of only saying that because he didn't like my family.

"That's not true, Alton," he said. "We just want you to succeed at Winfield, and I'm afraid something could happen that would prevent you from continuing down the positive path you've taken."

He had reason to worry, but I couldn't see that. I only knew I wanted to see my family. I wanted to hear them say they were proud of me for being the first person in our family to graduate from high school and for going on to college. I desperately wanted their approval; I also wanted them to support me the way I thought other families supported their college-bound sons and daughters.

Having said his piece, Phil said no more.

I drove to Stillwater, knowing my options were limited as to where I could stay. It came down to my mom's or my grandparents', but since I didn't know where my mom lived, I drove straight to my grandparents' house. The only person home was my grandma. I found her washing dishes in the kitchen.

"Hi, Grandma. I wanted to come see Mom and spend a few days with everyone before I leave for school."

Grandma didn't seem too excited to see me, but she did stop washing dishes long enough to make eye contact and tell me she was proud of me. She even patted me on the back, saying she always knew I could do it. It was rare praise from someone in my family, and hearing it made me glad I hadn't taken Phil's advice. Going home had been the right decision. Grandma said my mom was renting a small house near Ninth Avenue and West Street, and she'd love to see me. She made me promise that I would go by.

After our good-byes, I headed out the door. Across the street, kids played basketball and took turns on the big covered slide in the neighborhood park. It seemed such a far cry from when I had taken refuge there all those years ago after my Uncle Stevie threw me down the stairs. Yet I knew it wasn't. With broken ribs, my nine-year-old self had crawled under the cover of that very same slide and cried myself to sleep. The next morning, I had walked myself to DHS.

Aging Out

As I passed the park, I had to fight the tears back—not because of what Stevie had done to me all those years ago, but because of how alone I had felt that night. Seeing the park also triggered a wave of guilt for having left my family after that and, strangely, for having gotten Stevie arrested that night. I wondered how things would have been with them if I had stayed instead. Were my recent successes worth being ostracized by my family for so long, I wondered.

It would shock people to know that even then at age seventeen—after all they had done to me and all the times they had let me down, I would have cut off my right arm to have my family believe in me, love me, and be proud of me. As I drove away, I began to think that maybe they did love and believe in me, but I just couldn't see it. I started thinking that maybe there was something wrong with not them but me after all.

As the tears dried, I arrived at my mom's house, but she wasn't home. Not sure where to try next, I drove down the street a few blocks and spotted Mom and one of her friends standing in front of another house.

I pulled into the driveway and waved at my mom, and she and her friend greeted me as I got out of my car. Mom said she was glad to see me and even more thrilled that I had stopped by because she wanted to introduce me to someone.

With that, Mom turned, looked at the friend standing there with her, then back at me, and said, "Alton, I would like you to meet your Aunt Lucy."

"Nice to meet you, Lucy," I said.

The fact that I had no idea who this Aunt Lucy was nor had ever heard I had an Aunt Lucy before was irrelevant. Mom often introduced strange adults as my aunt or uncle. It was a Southern thing.

But then Mom said, "Alton, this is your dad's sister."

Speechless, I stared at my mom, as disappointment and confusion fought on my face. I noticed both Mom and Lucy seemed excited about sharing what to me was the ultimate revelation. I would not have been any more shocked had she told me that day my father was an alien. At least the latter would have explained why I had never had cause to meet, much less see, the man in seventeen years.

"It's nice to finally meet you, Alton," Lucy said.

Not knowing how to respond and all but incapable of doing so, I kept my mouth shut.

"He looks just like his dad," Lucy said, with a knowing smile.

"I told you so," said my mom, nodding her head.

If the two of them had expected a warm, cuddly, spontaneous family reunion, they were sadly mistaken.

I looked at my mom, and the pain had to have shone through my eyes as I said, "As far as I'm concerned, I do not have, nor have I ever had, a dad."

Before either could say another word, I jumped in my car and sped away. I know now that was the beginning of the fall.

The psychological boost my graduation had given me was fading. The fear that I was not up to what was to come at college was taking over. Depression had flung its dark blanket over me. Unbeknownst to me, I had been hanging on by the thinnest of threads all summer.

It was not the time to have my father become a reality . . . even in the harmless form of a friendly aunt.

My mother's news that day pushed me to the edge of the abyss.

I became an angry man that day.

And from that day forward, I would self-destruct many times before I got my life in order again.

I left Stillwater a very different person than the proud high school graduate who had driven in to town in his new car.

As I slunk back to Cushing, I wanted to hate my mom, yet somehow I just couldn't. Of course, I hadn't been able to hate her even when she made sure long ago that our relationship would never be what a mother and son should have.

That evening, I shared with Phil what had happened in Stillwater, and even though he had the right to say, "I told you so," to his credit, he didn't.

Chapter 8

Being a Foster Child

My mother's revelation about my father sent me into a tailspin, although I could not have told you that at the time. Looking back, it probably was inevitable because I had never dealt with what it meant to have been abandoned before I was even born by the man that society said had the right to call himself my father.

I have no memory of ever asking my mother where my dad was or why I didn't have one. My older brother, younger siblings, and cousins didn't have dads, so not having a father was all any of us knew. That was life. That was normal.

The only times it ever crossed my mind that I can recall were when I saw other kids' fathers doing things with or for them. I tried to imagine what that would be like, but I always came up empty. I don't know if I ever even said "Dad" or "Father" out loud before that July day with my mom and new aunt, and yet that encounter would unravel everything else for me.

To understand how I could let all the good slip away, it might help to understand better what it means to be a foster kid. I spent my formative years as a child in a home that would be considered by anyone as extremely dysfunctional. Although I knew somewhere in my soul that things were not as they should be in our home or my grandparents', that dysfunction was all I knew.

It was my normal. And that normal went with me wherever I went. It is what I compared the rest of the world against.

Being a foster kid can be explained like this:

Let's say my mother was a cat who raised a kitten. After several years, someone comes along and tells her she can no longer raise her kitten because she isn't doing it right. And so they remove her kitten and place the kitten with a friendly dog that has a litter of puppies. In the beginning, things are exciting and new, and the kitten likes having a full tummy and a warm place to sleep at night. Everything is different and so a bit scary, but the kitten does its best to fit in and act as the puppies act.

As time passes, however, the kitten eventually comes to realize that it is not like the puppies it lives with. Family photos, parent meetings at school, and expressions of familial love are constant reminders to the kitten that it is not one of the dog's puppies.

And then, one day, the kitten wakes up and realizes that no matter how hard it tries, the dog will never see it as a puppy. It will never be a puppy. The kitten always knew the dog and the puppies it lived with were not its family, the house it lived in was not its home, and the school it went to was not its school. Every time the kitten saw itself with the puppies, it hurt because deep down the kitten knew it was different. The kitten also knew that living with the dog and her puppies was better and safer, but still the kitten could not stop thinking about its mom and wondering how she was doing, if she missed her kitten, or wanted to see her kitten.

Thinking about such things can cause a foster kid to self-destruct and sabotage the good things going on in the child's life because once a kitten knows it will never ever be a puppy, what does it have left? It is simply a kitten living in a dog's world, which means it will never be able to relax and just be itself.

This is what a foster child fears to be true.

Chapter 9

Questions

As my senior year progressed, I had moments when I imagined what I would look like walking around the college campus wearing my backpack, sitting in class with other students, and playing football. But let me tell you a secret: I never saw myself as a sophomore.

Although I could imagine being a freshman in college, I could not see myself getting any farther. I simply didn't believe I had it in me to be a college graduate.

Those fears intensified and multiplied as the summer drew to a close and the time to leave for college grew near. I listened to other friends talk about how their parents were going to college to help them move into the dorms, get their schedules, and tour the campus. I knew that no one in my family would be by my side on my first day at Southwestern.

From the day I graduated from high school, I was afraid I wouldn't survive. I was afraid of being alone at college. I was literally terrified of college because I had no idea what I would find on campus, much less in the dorm, in the classroom, or on the football team. I had no idea who to go to for answers or help, and I wasn't about to randomly start asking teachers or classmates in Cushing because I didn't want anyone to think I was a clueless wimp. Neither Phil nor Marcy had gone to college, so I don't think it even occurred to them that I might be overwhelmed by the unknown that was college.

I kept my fears to myself and did what I could to convince everyone I knew that I had it under control, that I could make it.

Meanwhile, in the dark of night, I was asking myself a litany of questions, all of which began with: What if?

What if I fail all my classes?

What if I get sick?

What if I run out of money?

What if I can't find my classes?

What if I get the wrong textbooks?

What if I can't read well enough to understand the textbooks?

What if my roommate doesn't like me?

What if my professors don't like me?

What if my coach or teammates don't like me?

I tried to envision all these scenarios—and hundreds more—but I always came up blank. No one had passed on any of this knowledge or prepared me for what I was about to do. No one in my tribe had gone ahead to blaze a path for me to follow. I simply had no idea what to expect. I do remember my social worker from the Oklahoma Department of Human Services calling me right before it was time to leave for Kansas. "I want to take you shopping before you head to college," she said.

She came to Cushing, picked me up, and took me to Stillwater ,where she bought me school supplies, a backpack, and a small digital typewriter at Walmart, and then we headed to J. C. Penney for some school clothes and a pair of shoes.

When we were finished, she asked if I wanted to go by and see my family before we headed back to Cushing.

"I'd rather just go home," I said.

"Okay, Alton," she said.

Back at Phil and Marcy's, she helped me unload and carry the clothes and college supplies into the house, and then it was time for her to leave. It would be the last time I would ever see her; I was only about two months away from my birthday, when I would turn eighteen and age out of the foster care system.

"I'm extremely proud of you," she told me, "and you should be proud of yourself."

I walked her back to the car, thanked her for the supplies, gave her a hug, and watched her drive away. I appreciated what she'd said, but deep down I was afraid that my DHS worker was just one more person I would let down if I didn't do well in college.

Standing there, I also realized it was not her approval that I craved. What I wanted was someone from my own family to give me some credit for what I had accomplished and what I was about to do.

The pressure of being the first in my family to go to college, combined with going to school out of state and living by myself for the first time, was starting to build.

Chapter 10

College Boy

I was supposed to report to Kansas in late July 1988 for football. The day of my departure, Phil and Marcy helped me carry my few belongings to my car. I appreciated all they had done for me the past few years, yet my heart still ached, knowing it should have been my real mother and father wishing me well and seeing me off that day.

As I drove out of Cushing, I realized that in my seventeen years on this planet, I had lived in only two homes for more than three years, and Phil and Marcy's was one of them. The boys ranch was the other. My mom had lived in and been evicted from more houses than I could count. After that, I had lived in various foster and group homes in different towns.

I had grown up expecting to move every year—if not more often—and to expecting to have a stream of strangers come in and out of my life. I didn't know what permanence looked liked. And that meant I did not have the wherewithal to grasp what a four-year commitment to college meant. My upbringing had taught me not to think past a few days. I was stuck in the present. I might dream about being a good dad and stable husband who took care of his responsibilities, but I had no idea how to get there. Thinking about anything long term was not part of who I was because my entire life had been temporary.

Being unaware let me enjoy today.

It did not prepare me for what was to come. Truth be told, I had sabotaged college long before I ever made the trip to Winfield.

Everything I owned was in the back seat of my car, and I had probably twenty dollars on me—it was all I had. I was so nervous, I don't recall a single song on the radio during that two-and-a-half-hour drive; I only know the long drive gave me plenty of time to stoke my fears about what lay ahead. Did I have what it takes to be a college boy?

I was scared out of my mind as I drove my battered car onto the campus. I found plenty of empty parking spots, but having no idea where to go—the dorm? the athletic office? the registrar?—I wasted twenty minutes circling campus looking for a clue as to where I should be headed instead of taking a parking spot.

Finally, I rolled the dice and parked in front of what looked to be a dorm. Still uncertain, I stopped a stranger and asked where I needed to check in.

"If you're trying to check into your dorm," he said, "you should go there." He pointed to a big building on the other side of campus.

"If you're looking to get your class schedule, you should go there." And he pointed to a nearby building.

I thanked him, got out of my car, and headed toward the building that would get me my dorm room. Inside, I stood at the back, watching and hoping the stranger had sent me to the right place. Finally, convinced that the guy had been right, I joined a line and waited for my turn to find out what dorm I would be living in. I had almost relaxed when I realized the students at the front were showing an ID to the person at the counter. I reached down and felt my back pocket. No wallet. No ID. I stepped out of line, walked to the door, and then ran back to my car. Thankfully, my wallet, with my ID, was there; I grabbed them and headed back to the line to start the process all over again. When it was finally my turn, I prayed there wasn't something else I was supposed to have for check-in.

The lady at the counter didn't even raise her head: "Name?"

"My name is Alton," I said.

She looked up at me then, and said, "And what is your last name?"

"I'm sorry. My name is Alton Carter." I held my breath as she searched a stack of papers for my forms, wondering what I would do if she couldn't find mine. But after a few seconds, she located my name and took a small yellow envelope from a pile.

"This is your room key," she said, handing it to me. "Do your best not to lose it because if you do, you'll have to pay a fee to get another. Your dorm is next door. You should probably go check in."

I nodded and took the key. Funny, but just getting that room key made me breathe a little sigh of relief and gave me a much-needed boost of confidence.

As I walked back to my car and began to unload it, I couldn't help but notice that all the other kids moving in seemed to have parents with them. Dads and moms carried laundry baskets of clothes, bulletin boards and rolled posters, pillows and bedspreads, suitcases and boxes, radios and typewriters.

And there I was, alone.

I am not sure if anyone noticed that I was by myself, but in my mind, I imagined that everyone who passed saw me as the poor black kid—once again the foster kid with the big "F" burned into his chest, the one without a family.

Yet I know now that even if Phil and Marcy had been there that first day on campus, I'm pretty sure I would not have been happy. I wanted my real family to be there with me. I wanted my own mom to help me check into my dorm room, to help me purchase my meal card, to help me register and get my class schedule. I didn't want her because I needed her help. I just wanted her with me to share one of the most important days of my life.

When I finally made it up to my dorm room, there were three of us living in a room for two. I walked in, set my stuff on the bed in the middle of the room, and then sat on my bed watching my new roommates and their parents unload and unpack.

We must have exchanged words, but I don't recall any. All I

could think about was how much I hated the place. I wanted to go home, and I had not been on campus for more than a few hours. I was hurting, lonely, and scared of all the new things that were coming at me so fast.

Then I reminded myself, not for the first or the last time, that at least I had made it to college—that was something no one in my family had ever been able to do.

I was the first Carter ever to be a "college boy."

I liked the ring of that. I just hoped I could live up to it.

Chapter 11

Classes Begin

My first days on campus were all about football. I learned the routine of practice and team meals pretty easily, but the closer we got to classes starting, the more panicked I became.

The Southwestern campus didn't seem all that big to me, especially compared to OSU, and yet I struggled finding my way around and often got lost.

The first day of classes, I got completely turned around in all the people traffic. In class, I sat in the back and prayed no one would call on me. That became my routine, a matter of self-preservation.

Like that first question on the ACT exam, it took me only one class to realize I did not know how to take notes; I simply did not know what part of what the professor said was important. And it had taken me opening only one textbook to realize I was out of my element there as well.

Being in class caused me anxiety, and I also feared those big books.

The irony was that I was so proud to carry my books because they were what made me feel like a college student. The backpack, the student ID, the books, they all made me feel like I belonged at Southwestern. Sometimes I would carry all of my books at one time to class hoping to hide my fear from the world my fear of actually being asked to read them.

I didn't have a word at the time for why I had always found reading to be so difficult. If someone had asked me for one, I would have said, "I'm dumb." It would be years before I learned there was more to it than that.

Little wonder that my first college exam came back with a big, red "D" scrawled across the front. I had studied for hours for the test, poring over my notes, such as they were, and reading the assigned chapters as best I could.

When it came time to take the test, I was nervous but believed I was well prepared. I went straight to work on the questions, and time seemed to fly by. I stayed focused to the very end, and when I finally looked up, I realized everyone else had turned in their test and left. Still, I was confident and pretty sure I would get at least a "B."

When a few days later that "D" came back, I about died. I remember grabbing the test from my professor's hand, shoving it deep into my backpack, and praying that no one else had seen it.

My fear of both books and tests increased tenfold after that. How could I have been so wrong? To make matters worse, I also had no idea what I could have done to prepare better. Sometimes I heard kids in class or around the dorm talking about getting together in study groups before an exam, but I wanted nothing to do with that—too afraid of being the guy asking too many questions because I didn't understand the material.

It was obvious to me—and I'm sure to my professors—that I needed help, but my pride got the best of me. Instead of talking to my professor or getting a tutor or even attending the study groups, if only to listen, I did nothing. And in doing nothing, I sealed my fate.

Chapter 12

Reality Check

I wish I could say things were going better on the gridiron, but I'd be lying. I was one of many freshman players and really nothing more than a body and a number. And soon I had no idea what I was doing there either. Yet if it had not been for the athletic department staff, things could have been much worse—they were the ones who got my schedule and books for me at the start of school, and thanks to my football scholarship, I ate free in the dorm cafeteria and my textbooks were free.

Still, I had no money of my own, so when everyone went off campus to go bowling or to eat, I was left behind in the room. The others invited me; they just didn't know I was poor and couldn't afford to join them, and I wasn't about to tell them.

The end result was that I was left to my own devices. And my days came to be all the same, like that movie *Groundhog Day* with Bill Murray: I would get up early, eat breakfast, and go to class. In between classes, I'd eat lunch, and then after my last class, I was off to practice. Evenings, I did my homework and studied the team playbook.

Aging Out

It would be fascinating to know what those around me—my roommates, my coaches, my teachers—thought of me: Did I look like I knew what I was doing? Did I look like I had it all together? Or did I look like I was struggling as much as I was?

If they could have seen inside me, they would have known I was lost and wanted so badly to ask for their help. In the world of college sports, though, the last thing in the world a person wants to appear is weak. I wanted help, but what was I supposed to say, "Hey, Coach, I'm homesick"?

I certainly couldn't see myself going to my adviser or a counselor, if such a person even existed on campus, and saying that I was depressed, overwhelmed, and out of my element, much less confiding in anyone how much I hated myself.

Ashamed, I had convinced myself that I was the only freshman at Southwestern who was overwhelmed by college. I had no friends to tell me otherwise, either. That, I suspect, stemmed from my having no idea how to be a roommate. I had shared a room with people before in my life, but the reality of living with two strangers this time just added to my stress—I interacted so rarely with the two of them, I couldn't tell you their names.

Night was almost worse than day. I often could not sleep knowing that tomorrow would mean the return of the reality I feared most: college.

The idea of college had sounded so great back in Cushing in my dreams, and I had thought it would be fun, like the commercials you see on TV. I hadn't realized I was not prepared for any of it. I spent the next month or so going to class and practice, knowing that it was only a matter of time before I called it quits.

Most freshmen feeling lost or homesick would have found an excuse to go home to do laundry or spend a weekend or celebrate their birthday, but even if I had wanted to go home—even if my grandparents or mom would have had me—I couldn't afford to make the trip on a whim.

My eighteenth birthday came and went in late September without notice. I told no one, unwilling to have anyone else know my family had ignored or forgotten it.

I don't remember anyone else remembering it, either.

For a foster child, turning eighteen is a red-letter day. Yet I don't recall an exit interview or having to do any paperwork for DHS to gain my freedom. I'd seen a few boys turn eighteen while in foster care, and a lot left before then, eager to be on their own and making their own decisions. In fact, most of the kids I knew in foster care aged out prematurely. They either ran away before they turned eighteen or they just up and left the day they did.

In that way, foster kids are not so different from your ordinary eighteen-year-old: They know that the minute they turn eighteen, they are legally an adult, free to make their own decisions—good, bad, or indifferent—so long as they're willing to surrender the comfort of home should their parents not approve.

I think that's why aging out of the system for me always seemed akin to other kids turning of age. The choices we make from that moment on are ours and ours alone. Many of the foster kids I knew had a family member they could go live with when they aged out, but most of those who did returned to drug-riddled, abusive, or violent homes that almost guaranteed that the next time they were in court, it would be to be tried as an adult.

At least I had college. I saw that I had a choice. I had earned a scholarship and another four years of being someplace safe. I shouldn't have become a statistic. I know Phil and Marcy expected me to stay in school until the end, if only because I gave them no indication that I would do otherwise. I never considered leaving and going back to live with them because I didn't think it was an option. The state had paid them while I lived there as a foster kid. There would be no such stipend if I returned as an adult. They had done their part, and I didn't want to put a strain on their finances.

I had aged out. For better or for worse, I was on my own now.

Chapter 13

The Breaking Point

Fall break came, and it seemed like the entire campus was gone except for me. I was left alone to rattle about the dorm feeling sorry for myself for a good four days.

I know now that I stayed on campus over the break because it would later give me an excuse to justify my dropping out of college. It let me play victim. In reality, being alone for fall break was not the problem, nor was missing my family or thinking I wasn't smart enough. All those things were true, but the actual reason I left was because I gave up.

I gave up because all of the negative things that people—from my own uncles and siblings to my mother and grandmother—had always said about me started to slither back into my head like poisonous snakes.

For most of my life, I had told myself that I was not weak, scared, or a crybaby—or any of the other names my family had called me. Being unable to survive even one semester of college, however, was all the proof I needed that I was who they had always said I was. As for all the people who had said nice, positive things to me along the way, well, I convinced myself they had all lied to me. Why is it always so much easier for us to believe the bad about ourselves and not the good?

My decision, once made, was final: "I am leaving this place and never coming back."

I packed my stuff while my roommates were in class and left without saying a word to them, my coaches, or my teachers.

I didn't give any of them a chance to help me through whatever it was that I was going through.

As far as I was concerned, no one in the world could ever understand what I was feeling, so I headed south back to Stillwater, leaving behind the only thing I had going for me.

I have heard it said that most people aren't afraid of failure; they're afraid of success. I know only that almost from the day I arrived at Southwestern, I saw myself as a failure—before I even gave myself a chance to succeed. I suspect my life had made me more comfortable with failure.

The drive home was the longest car ride I had ever made, and for some reason, it seemed strangely unfamiliar to me. More than once, I wondered if I was going the right way. Maybe that was my heart trying to tell me I wasn't supposed to go home.

Unfortunately, I didn't listen. I just kept driving, all too willing to give up all I had accomplished. I did have second thoughts. A few miles outside Winfield, it suddenly occurred to me that maybe it was not too late to turn around—maybe I could get back and put my stuff up before anyone realized I had tried to bail, before anyone could call me a quitter.

Yet even as those thoughts swirled through my head, even as I realized that returning made more sense than leaving, I kept driving south—into uncertainty.

In hindsight, I believe the reason was unfinished family business. For the first time, even though not one of them had ever visited or called me at college, I felt as though my family in Stillwater was reaching out to me, and I could not say no.

I felt as if I owed them something, that leaving school would make up for the night I had called the police on Uncle Stevie and left them all those years ago. In my misguided reasoning, my leaving college was the price of their love.

I rehearsed in my head what I would say to them: Look what I gave up for you. Doesn't this prove how much I love all of you? I gave up a college scholarship to come back home and be part of this family.

To the outside world, I looked like a big, strong young man with his whole life ahead of him.

Inside, I was still a kitten, craving to return to its own kind.

Going home—returning in a way that my family couldn't reject me—was worth any sacrifice, even my future.

I was just running away again, but I told myself that this time, I was running *to* something.

For the first time in a long time, I felt in control.

I drove the last leg of the trip with purpose in my heart.

I never turned around.

I never pumped the brakes.

I just kept barreling south to home.

Chapter 14

Facing the Music

Despite all the happy family reunions I had imagined on my return, I knew they would not include my grandfather. Grandpa Carter was going to be hurt and upset at my news. I went through the excuses I would use to help him understand why I had left school. I knew none of them would ring true.

I rolled into Stillwater, knowing that no one in the family knew I was coming. I circled the town thinking about where I could go. There were only two places for me to stay. I could stay at my grandparents' house and deal with my grandpa being upset about my dropping out of school or I could find out where my mom was living and see if I could stay with her.

The decision wasn't that hard to make.

I decided to face the music with my grandpa, and I pointed the car toward their neighborhood.

I had made up my mind that I would tell my grandpa I just wasn't smart enough for college, but when I arrived at the house, he was nowhere to be found. I found Grandma downstairs watching television.

Aging Out

"Why are you in Stillwater?" she asked.

"I'm home for fall break," I lied. "Where's Grandpa?"

"He's reffing an out-of-town game; he'll be home late."

Claiming to be tired from the drive, I went upstairs under the guise of taking a nap. I spent all night trying to predict how my grandpa was going to respond.

*****

The next morning, I found Grandpa in the front yard working on his old truck. He stopped me before I could say a thing.

"Your coach called me and told me you dropped out," he said.

I started to offer up my prepackaged excuse, but he stopped me again. "I don't want to hear it, Alton. I'm disappointed in you. You've made a bad choice, but it's not too late to go back."

He looked at me. I shook my head.

"Well, then, you need to leave because I'm not going to let you stay here."

He looked so sad as he turned away. "I had hoped you'd be different than all the others," he said, quietly.

As I walked to my car, Grandpa called out after me one last time. "Alton, if you're smart, you'll get a job."

I didn't know it then, but in refusing me a place to land, my grandpa was trying to protect me, trying to force me to stand on my own. But that morning, all I heard was, "I don't want you."

It is amazing how a wounded heart will sometimes take truth and make it into a lie. For years, I had told myself I didn't want to be like everyone else in my family, but I think I always believed the adage that blood is thicker than water. Their blood ran in my veins—how could I escape that?

Broken and accepting my fate, I went to my mom's, only to realize that was more than even I could handle.

Her rented house was small, filthy, and swarming with roaches. I don't remember a warm welcome from her, just my own realization that I could no more stay the night there than I could have bathed in a tub of eels.

I left my bags at her house and headed over to the house of one of my friends from childhood. I kept it casual, like I just happened to be in town visiting and wanted to catch up. The last thing I wanted was for anyone to feel sorry for me, and I certainly didn't want anyone to know I didn't have a place to sleep that night, much less live.

I stayed on the move for the next few days, and over the course of my wanderings, one of the first people I ran into was my Uncle Stevie.

"Well, well, well," he said, "look who it is, the college boy who thinks he's better than all the rest of us."

Every family member I ran into in those first days back in town had a similar welcome for me. It was most decidedly not what I had hoped for on my return. I had thought things would go down differently. I thought they would be glad to see me and do all they could to make things right between us.

I thought, being a failure now myself, a dropout just like them, that I would be welcomed back into the fold. Instead, it was as if I had given them a new taunt to torment me with to add to all the old ones.

In fact, I realize now, they were welcoming me into their world. Their world was a dark, self-destructive place where people hurt and cursed and enabled each other, pointing out each other's flaws for the enjoyment of whoever happened to be around, flaming the fires of insecurity so that no one ever dared venture outside in search of a better life.

My mom and my uncles and my grandma should have told me to get my butt back to college and make something of myself, but misery loves company. My failing at college just proved to them they'd been right not to even try.

Chapter 15

Homeless

In less than two months, I had gone from college boy to college dropout, from having a dorm room and a comfy bed to sleeping on the couch of mere acquaintances, from having a bright future to not knowing where my next meal was going to come from.

I was a former foster kid.

I had just turned eighteen.

And I was homeless.

I had become the statistic I had tried so hard to avoid.

According to Covenant House, nearly 40 percent of foster kids who age out of foster care will spend some time living on the streets or couch-surfing. In a country where most parents would go to the ends of the earth to find a son or daughter who had gone missing, that is a difficult statistic to get your head around. Yet it is the norm for foster kids, and in that, I was no exception.

As far as I can recall, no one ever came looking for me. In that respect, I was living everyone's worst fear—whether you're a foster kid or not, a fear almost worse than the fear of being homeless:

I had been forgotten.

Being forgotten is normally a hazard of dying, but I was very much alive, and so it bore a hole so deep in my heart and psyche that more than twenty years later, I am still trying to fill it.

Of course, I did not know that then.

I was too busy trying to survive.

In the beginning, my efforts in that regard were helped by three things: I had my car, Stillwater is a pretty safe and small college town, and it was fall in Oklahoma—temperatures were neither too hot nor too cold. I might not have money for gas or a burger or a hotel room, but if worse came to worst I could safely live and sleep in my car. I had shelter of a kind.

And then one day, not too long after returning to Stillwater, a few of my friends and I decided to go play basketball across town. We jumped in my car and headed to a park where we had played several times before. We were almost there when I noticed red, white, and blue lights flashing in my rearview mirror. It was my first time to be pulled over by the police, so I was not sure what to do. My friends were no help.

"You're being pulled over for being black," one said.

"Yeah, he's going to get you for driving while black," said another.

I wasn't sure if what my friends said was true or not. My only memories of law enforcement came from my childhood back when I lived with my grandparents, and I remembered that even the time the police had come running in response to my own 9-1-1 call for help, the encounter had ended with my grandma on the porch screaming obscenities at both me and the cops. I slept in the park that night and left home the next day. Anyone who had witnessed that encounter would not have been able to tell you who the good or bad guys were.

The officer came to my window and asked for my license and registration. With hands shaking, I handed him both items.

"I'll be back in a minute," he said.

He walked back to his patrol car, leaving me to worry about what might happen next.

My thoughts raced while every bad encounter my family had ever had with the police played on a loop in my head. I just knew the officer was calling for backup and that at any minute, more squad cars would arrive on the scene and somebody would demand that we all get out of the car. My friends and I would be searched, separated, and asked all sorts of questions—and that was if everything went well. If any one of us mouthed off or resisted their orders, TV news told me, we would find ourselves facedown, cuffed, and spread-eagled on the ground—headed for jail.

And then, just like that, the officer was back at my window alone.

"Mr. Carter, do you know that you are driving around with an expired driving permit?"

"No, sir," I lied, hoping that if I played stupid, it might get me out of trouble.

The officer frowned.

"Mr. Carter, do you know that your insurance is expired as well?"

Again, I played stupid and said, "No officer, I thought it was up to date."

I noticed my friends had gone cold quiet.

The officer's expression remained calm and professional.

"Well, Mr. Carter, we have a problem because by law, you should not be driving, as you do not have a valid driver's license or insurance. Technically, I could take you to jail, but today I'm going to give you a break. I'm going to write you two citations: one for the invalid driver's license and one for driving without car insurance."

He handed me the tickets.

"Since your license is expired, you cannot drive your car anymore."

He went on to say that since I didn't have car insurance at the time of the stop, more than likely my license, once I got it, would be suspended. The officer then asked if anyone else in the car had a license, and one of my friends said he did. After showing it to the officer, my friend traded places with me, and we were allowed to leave.

As we drove away, I told my friends I could not believe the officer had been so nice. Looking back, I realize he had been both respectful—calling me Mr. Carter, despite my being barely an adult—and professional—explaining what I had done wrong and what was likely to happen going forward. It was a far cry from watching my relatives being hauled away kicking and screaming and in handcuffs and shoved into the back of a police car. Those were the memories of a little boy who never understood why the police were at our house or why anyone was being arrested. Even years later, after I was grown, it never occurred to me that the police might have been responding at those times to how my relatives responded to them. I wonder now how things might have gone if my uncles had only once gone along with the police peacefully.

It was now clear to me that my opinion of law enforcement came from what I had been taught and what, as a child, I had overheard my family members say about police. I had been taught that the police were the enemy. I had heard everyone, including my grandma, curse the police. And it surely had not helped matters that the one encounter I, myself, ever had with the police—as a boy caught joy-riding on a stolen bicycle on the OSU campus—ended with a police officer putting a gun to my head in attempt, he claimed, to try to scare me straight.

This officer, the one who took my license, couldn't have been more different than that campus policeman. I look back on that traffic stop as one of those times in life when you realize how wrong it is to generalize about people, to lump all police officers together, to judge all cops by one bad cop.

What if this officer had judged me based on a few bad encounters with other young black men? What if he hadn't extended professional courtesy to me just because I was a kid? I was worldly enough to know that our simple traffic stop could have gone horribly wrong—for everyone.

A few months later, I stopped by to visit my grandparents, and Grandpa greeted me with a letter from the Department of Motor Vehicles informing me that my driver's license was suspended. To get it back, I would have to pay a large fine.

I had no more finished reading the letter than my grandpa held out his hand. "Give me the keys to the car," he said.

I reached in my pocket for the keys, handed them over, and left the house on foot. Once again, I saw in my grandpa's eyes how much I had disappointed him.

Chapter 16

The 1 Percent

If you've never been homeless, you may not realize there are degrees of homelessness. When I still had my car, I was like the 1 percent— better off than the other 99 percent of homeless people. When I lost my car, I became more vulnerable, but my age, my gender, and the university community I lived in kept me numbered among the lucky.

In fact, until writing this book, I had not once ever out-and-out said I was once "homeless."

I simply could not say the word.

Homeless.

What about that word is so scary to someone like me, someone brave enough as a little kid to walk away from his family at age nine, who shuttled between foster homes and a boys ranch for years, who grew up in a family where people either overdosed, died, or went to prison? I'm still trying to figure that one out.

I can only tell you that those years after leaving Southwestern were so traumatic that my first draft of this book left them all out. I had buried those memories, like people sometimes do when something is too painful to remember.

It took a great effort to pull memories from that black hole, partly because every day back then was all but the same. I hated Christmas and spent it by myself; I did my best to make it like every other day because I knew there would be no present or card or Merry Christmas for me. My eighteenth birthday, the one that would see me step off alone into the unknowable abyss that was my future, no card, no phone call, certainly no gifts or cake.

Asking me to describe those years is a lot like asking a prisoner to describe life in jail. You describe one day, you've described them all.

And yes, it is torture when you realize that you have lost what should have been some of the best days and most vivid days of your life.

*****

As I've said before, finding a place to crash each night or grabbing a free meal was made easier thanks to Stillwater being a college town. I'd walk to campus for a pickup game of basketball and then tag along with whoever would give me a ride when the guys decided to go get something to eat after the last game.

I learned to make sure I arrived at people's houses or dorms around mealtime—otherwise, I didn't eat. If I was with someone and that person stopped somewhere to get a snack or meal, I would either ask to borrow a few bucks, act like I wasn't hungry, or pretend I'd left my wallet somewhere.

Most of the time, my ruse worked, but not always. One night after playing basketball, several of us piled into a car and headed off campus to McDonald's. Standing single file inside waiting to order, I made sure to stay at the back of the line. As the other guys one by one placed, paid, and got their orders, I stared at the dollar menu as if still trying to decide what to get. When I could delay no longer, I stopped one of the guys and asked if I could borrow two dollars.

"I promise I'll pay you back," I told him.

Without hesitation, he reached in his pocket and pulled out a five-dollar bill. Full of guilt but too hungry to do anything but continue the charade, I took the money, turned back to the cashier, and ordered as much food as I could get for five bucks. My skin still crawls with shame when I think of that exchange. That guy who I borrowed the money from? I didn't even know his name.

Eighteen-year-olds eat often and a lot, mostly because they're still growing—turning from gangly youngsters into muscular, solid men. I've heard more than one say he could eat all day and still be hungry. After leaving Southwestern, I was starving more times than not. At a time when the college kids around me were being challenged to discover their best selves, to broaden their minds, and to expand their horizons, I was reduced to my most basic animal needs: how to get food, water, and shelter.

Once after I hadn't eaten for two days, I was so weak I almost passed out while walking across town to a friend's. The more I walked, the hungrier I became. Finally, I had to stop. I knew I needed food but had no idea where to get any. After sitting under a shade tree for a few minutes, I remembered a nearby bakery known to regularly throw out its expired baked goods in a dumpster behind the store. I picked myself up and walked back to the bakery.

Not wanting to look suspicious, I first casually walked past the trash bin v to make sure there was something inside worth grabbing. I was in luck—the dumpster was half full of bread, doughnuts, and pies still in their packages.

I decided my best option was to circle back around so I could make sure no one was looking before I helped myself to the food. I knew I couldn't be picky or spend a lot of time digging for the best stuff or I would get caught. It's not illegal to dumpster-dive in most places in this country unless there is a local ordinance against it (you can thank the U. S. Supreme Court for that), but if you're on private property, you can get arrested for trespassing. By this time, I knew enough to be careful.

After making sure no one was looking, I returned to the trash bin, reached in, grabbed a loaf of raisin bread and a box of powdered doughnuts, and quickly walked away.

As soon as I was around the corner and out of sight of any employee taking a break, I opened the bread, grabbed a slice, and started to eat. The growl in my stomach slowly quieted, and I packed up and headed to my friend's, finishing the entire bag of baked goods before I arrived.

Being hungry drove me to do things I wasn't proud of doing—from dumpster-diving to mooching off friends to eating in dorm cafeterias on someone else's meal ticket—but I preferred to beg, borrow, or steal from others than ask my family for anything.

I know it sounds misguided, maybe a little crazy, even, but I was a young man, and I had my pride. The fact that what mattered to me was not what the world thought about me—or what the people I hung around thought of me—is telling.

It speaks to the power of familial ties.

It speaks to how much we want to please our mother and father, impress our brothers and sisters, make proud our grandparents—those we love can hold such power over us. Those who come before us show us the way, good or bad. Those who come along with us help keep us on the path, good or bad.

To step off that path, to deny that example, is to deny one's family.

No wonder I blocked out those years.

Chapter 17

The Pursuit of *Happyness*

If there was any sign that I might still make it in that year or two after I left Southwestern, it was probably the same personal habit that director Gabriele Muccino deemed to include in the film *The Pursuit of Happyness*. Remember how Will Smith as single father Chris Gardner each night washes out his white dress shirt until it is spotless, even as he and his son find themselves living first in a shelter and then in a subway bathroom?

That was me.

It is another good thing I took away from what were some otherwise brutal days at the Lions Boys Ranch in Perkins: the importance of cleanliness and good grooming.

I hated being dirty, and I had developed the discipline to make sure I never was.

If I were couch-surfing at a friend's house that had a washing machine, I would ask if I could put my clothes in with his. If there were no washing machine and I needed something clean to wear, I would either borrow something from the friend or wash my clothes in his bathtub.

I had seen my grandma wash clothes in the tub many times, so I knew exactly how to do it. The secret is to run enough water in the tub to submerge all the clothes, let the clothes soak in the water until wet through and through, and then use a bar of soap to scrub each garment until they all are full of suds. Let the clothes sit again for a few minutes. After that, drain the tub, turn on the faucet, and rinse each item under the water one by one until all the soap is gone.

After all my clothes were rinsed, I would twist them one item of clothing at a time until I had removed as much water from each garment as possible. Finally, I would hang the clothes on the shower curtain rod so they could dry.

Ironically, good hygiene and being well groomed are among the things that an employer first notices in a job applicant, especially if you don't have any other experience. If I had only known that then, what a difference it would have made in my life!

The problem was that while I was sparkling clean and, as far as the world was concerned, attractive on the outside, my messy insides made me feel like the unwashed, someone no one would take a chance on—certainly not a business owner.

By this time, it has probably become quite clear that being homeless is a time-sucking state of being—and labor intensive. I walked while others drove. I washed clothes by hand while others tossed theirs into a machine or did them at a Laundromat. I waited until the late late movie on TV ended so I could stay the night on someone's couch without drawing comment, while others simply went to bed when they were sleepy.

Luckily, those first few years back in Stillwater, I never had a place to be, so my time came cheap. I wasted hours waiting for someone to catch a ride with, for someone to get hungry so I could bum a bite to eat, for someone to do their wash so I could throw mine in, too.

It was no way for anyone to live.

And it only got worse if, God forbid, you fell sick or got injured.

Despite my poor nutrition, I don't remember getting sick very often—I credit the walking and my youth. However, I did get hurt a few times playing sports. I lacked a regular doctor, so I went to the emergency room for small things, for big things, for everything. One afternoon after a game of basketball, I got a sharp pain in my hip and was having difficulty walking and bending over. The pain wasn't killing me but it was constant, and I thought I'd developed a hernia.

My response: I had one of the other players take me to the emergency room at the Stillwater hospital because I didn't have the money to go to a doctor. That was what I had always seen my family members do as a child. That is what I did after aging out and being left on my own. That is what I did in 1989, the year my Social Security records show I earned a total of $769.

After several years, I owed the hospital what to me seemed like a ton of money. I had no idea how to open a checking account, much less how one went about getting health insurance. I never went to the dentist either.

And once again, I told myself I would rather suffer in pain or rack up a pile of medical bills or have my teeth rot than have my mom take care of me like my grandma had her sons. I did not want to be like my uncles, grown men without jobs living at home in a house paid for by the toil of their parents.

I just didn't know how to be anything else.

Chapter 18

The Shadow

There was another reason I could not turn to my mother. Like the name that shall not be spoken, for most of my life, it has been too dark and too horrible to be said aloud, much less brought into the light of day.

My heart is broken because of a man who helped create me but who refused to be my dad.

My heart is battered because of a family that persecuted me for trying to be a good man.

And my heart is forever bruised because of a mother who did to me what no mother should do to a son.

I don't write this to have people feel sorry for me or to brand my mother as a terrible person but rather to have others see how God brought me through all the shadows, how it is possible to endure the unspeakable.

People often ask me how I turned out the way I did because by everything we know, I should not be here today. I should not be who I am today. I made it because not only was God with me, but also because I knew He was with me. I made choices that set me apart from my family. It is difficult to explain, but I knew as a young boy that I was not going to live a life of crime.

When I was young, several things happened in my life that caused me to want to be different.

Some of them I take pride in.

Others I wish had never happened.

The "Shadow" is one I would banish from my childhood if only I had the power.

The Shadow, you see, stole my nights.

My first memory of the Shadow is of a shape hovering outside the living room where I slept on the couch. I couldn't see its face, but I knew who it was. Each time the Shadow lay beside me, it told me not to tell anyone about its visit.

I can't remember the physical part that accompanied that request because at that warning, my mind went to a different place, leaving my body behind, leaving me to feel betrayed and ashamed of who and what I was.

The mornings after a visit by the Shadow brought more shame. I found it difficult to look into the face of my mother and found it even harder to look at myself in the aftermath. I will never know what the nights of other children are like, but I knew then, and I know now, that what I endured in the dark of those nights was wrong.

I just did not understand how to make it stop.

I took to finding any excuse to stay over at a friend's house, but the price of that was guilt. I had never told my younger brothers and sister about the Shadow, and so I felt guilty because I wasn't there to protect them. Did the Shadow visit them when I was away?

My implosion at college and the lost years that followed my return to Stillwater are proof that you can't bury some things, like the Shadow, like an absentee father, like an abusive childhood, and expect them to stay buried.

To lay them to rest, so you can get on with life, you have to shine the light on them.

But I did not know that then.

And because I did not know that, I aged out of the foster care system in Oklahoma only to find myself stuck in a dark whirlpool of regret. I felt the need to keep my dark secrets close, holding my resentment even closer.

It would have been a personal loss for me if this time had only spanned my summer after high school or my two months at Southwestern or my first year back in Stillwater.

But I was homeless for almost four years.

What finally changed my life was a bike . . . and a girl.

Chapter 19

Self-Sufficiency

It's hard to believe, but I don't remember how I came to acquire the bicycle. I don't know if someone gave me it or lent it to me, but overnight, I was mobile again, self-sufficient. I quickly went from pedaling it to get around town, instead of walking or bumming rides, to deciding it was the ticket to getting to work.

There was only one catch: I didn't have a job, and I had no idea how to go about getting one.

Unfamiliar with things like résumés and vitae, I did what most people in my situation would do—I saw signs on local fast-food restaurants saying they were hiring and asked how to apply. I was so relieved when they said all I needed to do was fill out a one-page application. I could do that.

It didn't go well at first. It took a few weeks to get my first job at Long John Silver's, and it lasted only a few days thanks to a personality conflict with the manager. My next attempt was at the local McDonald's; I got a part-time job for minimum wage, about $4.25 an hour, and a free meal per shift. My shift was opening the restaurant, which meant I was to be at work ready to work at 5:00 a.m. sharp.

The first thing I did every morning was make the biscuits and gravy. I moved on to working at the grill frying sausage, ham, and eggs or manning the fryer making hash browns. McDonald's was a great place to work, and I liked my fellow employees and the manager, a supernice guy with a good attitude. I was grateful for the job.

McDonald's has rules to make sure food stays fresh and hot, and so whether it's a burger or a biscuit, the wrapper on the item gets a time stamp. If that item is not sold by that time, it is supposed to go straight to the trash.

By now, however, despite the resentment I felt for my mother and what she had done to me as a child, I felt the need to take care of her, and so I was trying to keep both of us fed. It killed me to see what looked like perfectly good food thrown in the trash. So instead of following protocol, I started to collect expired food in a sack that I hid in the back of the restaurant until I got off work.

I hated sneaking around, but I justified my actions by saying the food was going in the trash anyway, so it shouldn't matter if I took it home. Deep down, I knew it was stealing, but I was so hungry—and so was my mom.

After several months, I quit McDonald's for the promise of a better job. I was making progress, but some days it seemed like two steps forward and one step back. I was still couch-surfing, and a lot of my days were still spent playing basketball on one of the four courts at the OSU Annex. The games drew college students, locals, and athletes from the area. Through the years, I had made several friends from those games, and they were often the ones who gave me rides, fed me, and shared their hand-me-down clothes with me.

One afternoon while waiting for my turn to play, I overheard one of the regulars mention that he was looking for a roommate, someone willing to pay two hundred bucks a month in rent to share the house his parents had purchased for him while he went to school. I told him I was looking for a place and asked if I could come see the house.

Scott gave me a ride to his house, and I quickly told him that I'd like to stay there, even though I knew I didn't have the money for rent. He wasn't asking for a security deposit or anything, so I asked if it was okay to pay the first month's rent at the end of the month. He said okay, and I moved in.

At the end of the month, I did not have the money.

When Scott asked for it, I told him it was coming, and I would get it to him the next day. A few days later, I borrowed forty dollars from a friend and gave it to Scott. He set it on his desk in his room and thanked me for trying to pay something, and then he told me I would have to pay the rest by the end of the week or I would have to move out.

Even as I agreed, I knew I would not have the money then either, so when the end of the week came, I decided to leave before he could ask me for it. I packed my few bags and went into his room, took back my forty dollars that was still on his desk and left without saying a word. I knew taking the money was wrong but I was once again in survival mode.

For several more months, I continued my routine of shuffling between the houses of friends at night and playing basketball at the Annex by day. Eventually, I met a guy named Kenny, a freshman at OSU, studying to be an accountant.

After running into Kenny a few times at the Annex, we became friends and started to spend quite a lot of time together. Kenny was a neat kid with a big heart, and I eventually felt comfortable enough to share with him a little about my situation.

"I don't really have a place to live," I told him.

Without hesitation, Kenny told me I could stay with him.

I didn't even think to ask where he lived; instead, I asked him to take me by my mom's house to pick up a few of my things.

Come to find out Kenny lived on the tenth floor of a dorm on the OSU campus, but he happened to be good friends with the floor's resident assistant, so he didn't anticipate any problems. He also didn't have a roommate, which meant there was an empty bed in his room.

For the next few months, Kenny's dorm room became home for me. More than once, he let me use his meal plan so I could eat. Eventually, I was spending enough time on campus that I figured out other places that I could sneak into for a free meal. Kenny and

I went almost everywhere together, and he never complained about footing the bill. I'll never forget him—or his red Nissan 240 and its awesome sound system.

Chapter 20

I Meet Kristin

About the same time the bike came into my life, a girl did, too. I might have blocked out most of that time in my life, but I remember the moment I met Kristin.

My buddies were in the middle of a game at OSU's Colvin Center instead of its adjacent annex, and this particular day, I wasn't playing. Instead, I had taken a seat on the sidelines to watch my friends play.

Like the annex, the Colvin Center had four basketball courts, with two places from which to watch the games—on the floor or upstairs in a long balcony. I decided to go upstairs so I could watch all four games being played at once. I was halfway up the stairs when I saw a girl with long blonde hair sitting cross-legged on the floor, watching her friends play ball. I still remember what she was wearing—hot pink shorts and a white T-shirt with pink letters. Any interest in the games themselves disappeared.

I walked down the hallway toward her, and when I was a few feet away, I caught her eye.

"Will you marry me and have ten kids?" I asked.

With a look of shock on her face, she quickly turned her attention back to the game she had been watching.

Almost two decades later, Kristin and I both agree those were the first words out of my mouth on meeting her for the first time. But she insists they were spoken at a local dance hall called Tumbleweeds, not at the Colvin Center.

The way I remember it, however, I sat down next to her that day in the balcony while our friends played ball below, and we talked and talked. I learned she was in her freshman year at OSU. Her dad worked for Williams Natural Gas, and her mom was a homemaker. She had an older sister named Kelly and a younger brother, Cole, who was born with Down syndrome. The more I talked to Kristin, the more I realized that she was too smart and too good for me. I couldn't see her ever agreeing to go out with me.

Yet instead of trying to up my game so I did deserve her, I opted to lie to her about everything.

I told her I was a sophomore at OSU and that my parents were divorced. I told her my dad lived in Texas and my mom lived in Stillwater. We talked for hours that day, and I got her dorm phone number before she left.

Over the next few months, we talked often on the phone, and I managed to run into her from time to time. I wanted to impress her but feared that if she found out the truth about me, she would have nothing to do with me.

At the time, I was in between couches so had been staying with my mom, but I told Kristin I was living with a friend in an apartment a few blocks off campus. I figured it was best to lie about my address because I knew it was only a matter of time before she found out I wasn't enrolled in college. If she ever happened to come by to pick me up or drop me off, I would have her do so in front of this one apartment building. Only when she was out of sight, would I walk to my mom's house, just behind the complex.

I asked Kristin out more than once before she finally agreed to go on a date with me. Having been turned down several times already, I was shocked when one day after hanging out I asked again, and she said yes.

"I want to take you to the movies tonight, so be ready about nine," I said.

"Do you want me to come pick you up?" she asked.

"No, I'll come by your dorm, and we can go from there."

I had refused her offer of a ride because I didn't want her to figure out I didn't have an actual address. And by eight o'clock, I was second-guessing myself for having asked her out. I didn't have money for movie tickets nor anyone to borrow the money from that night.

And so I was a no-show.

I hung out with a friend instead, and spent the whole night thinking of Kristin.

A few days later, I ran into Kristin, and she was quick to remind me how I had stood her up. I made up some lame excuse to justify what I'd done, but I could see the reason didn't matter.

"The least you could have done was call, Alton," she said.

She was right. I should have called. I should also have been honest with her as to why I didn't show that night, but I was too insecure to do either. Often my reasoning on things didn't even make sense to me. I was torn between telling her I had no place to live and no money or just keeping it a need-to-know secret.

After several apologies and my begging for a second chance, she agreed to go out with me again.

"But if you stand me up again, there won't be another," she said.

I promised it wouldn't happen again, and a few days later, we made it to the movies. Luckily, Kenny was back in town, and I'd been able to borrow the needed cash from him.

At the movies, I was too nervous to try to hold her hand—afraid it might be too much, too soon. I settled for watching the movie with her. Afterward, Kristin offered to take me home, but I countered with the suggestion that we return to her dorm and I would walk home from there. We must have stood talking for an hour outside her residence hall when I suggested a walk. We headed off and soon found ourselves at a small park south of campus, where we sat in the swings and talked and laughed as if we'd known each other forever.

The world stood still for me that night.

And it made me face a harsh truth: I was still lying to Kristin, at least about my status as a college student. She thought I was a sopho-more studying to be a physical education teacher because that is what I had told her. Oh, the things we do to avoid rejection.

It was nearly two in the morning when we said our good-byes. We parted with a hug at the dorm door, she went up to her room, and I went to Kenny's. I should have slept well on the memories of a second first date gone so well, but instead I lay awake ashamed, ashamed that I had spent most of the night spinning a whole bunch of new lies for Kristin's consumption.

Would she like me if she knew the truth?

I could only wonder.

Chapter 21

Picnic with Kristin

Almost everywhere Kristin and I went together, she drove because I didn't have a car. One afternoon, she asked if I would like to go on a picnic with her.

"Sounds fun," I said. "I've never been on a picnic before."

She looked at me like she thought I was teasing, but I wasn't. My family didn't do picnics, neither had any of my foster parents, and so all I knew about them was what I had seen on television: two people on a blanket with a bottle of champagne and a picnic basket full of sandwiches in the middle of a field somewhere. It had always seemed nice, what many people would call romantic, but I had never dreamed I would ever be on a picnic with someone special.

When Kristin picked me up the day of our picnic, I was both nervous and excited. She drove us east to the edge of town to Couch Park and found an empty place to leave the car. She unloaded a sack of groceries and handed me a blanket, and we walked to a shady, leafy spot away from the noise of the nearby playground.

I unfolded the blanket and placed it on the ground, and we both found ourselves a spot on it and, for a quiet moment, took in all the trees and blooming wildflowers. Kristin impressed me by identifying several trees and plants. Time passed quickly.

After we had chatted for a while, she asked, "Are you hungry?"

"Yes," I said. "What have you got in there?"

She pulled out a loaf of bread, packages of sliced ham and cheese, a jar of mayonnaise, a bag of chips and another of grapes, and two cans of Sprite. While she made the sandwiches, I opened the chips and pop. We chatted some more as we devoured our picnic lunch.

By the time the last chip was gone, I felt as if I was beginning to get the hang of this picnic thing. And I surprised even myself when I got the idea to make a necklace for Kristin out of the clover growing all through the park.

I circled the blanket on my knees searching for just the right blooms. Once I had gathered enough, I returned to the blanket next to Kristin and began to weave the blooms together for her necklace, using my fingernail to make a small slit near the bottom of the stem, then threading the stem of the next bloom through until the petals stopped it.

I repeated this process, adding one clover at a time, until I had made a necklace long enough that it would fit over her head. I had done it simply to impress the girl I liked, and I knew it wasn't much—it wasn't made of silver or gold, but Kristin acted like it was a big deal and told me how much she liked it.

With her necklace around her neck, Kristin and I spent hours more in the park, talking and people-watching and enjoying being outside. I sure hated to see it end, but eventually the sun slipped beneath the horizon and it began to get dark, so we loaded the car and headed home.

Outside my sham address, I kissed her good-bye and watched as she drove away. I felt closer to Kristin in that moment than to anyone I had ever known. I wanted nothing more than to spend as much time with her as possible for as long as possible, ideally forever. As her taillights disappeared into the night, I could only hope that she felt the same way about me, but truthfully, I wasn't sure. Despite all the time we had now spent together, I still couldn't help but wonder if she truly cared about me or just felt sorry for me. Those emotions can look alike sometimes. As for me, I wondered if what I felt for her was true love or simply gratitude for her being so kind to me.

Either way, I knew one thing for certain: I wanted as much of Kristin's time as she was willing to share with me.

In the weeks and months that followed, I came to believe I was in love with Kristin. Yet I feared if I told her so, she would leave, move away, and break my heart—just like my first girlfriend, Jamie, had done all those years ago back in high school in Cushing.

Still, I could not stop how I felt about Kristin or keep my love for her from growing, and eventually I came to accept that she was the one for me. I just wasn't sure if I was the one for her. And I wasn't sure if love would be enough.

She was white and I was black. It was the 1990s, but I knew some people would have a problem seeing us together. There were obstacles ahead, and I wondered if we would be able to weather them.

That said, I knew, whether we ended up together or eventually parted, I would always be grateful to Kristin. Most all of what I know about love and what a healthy relationship looks like, I learned from her.

Chapter 22

A Break in the Clouds

I didn't see my family much in those days, but as fate would have it, one day while I was playing basketball in a city park, a distant cousin approached me about a job.

Carl Connor had grown up in Stillwater and loved gymnastics. After he graduated from Stillwater High, he began to teach gymnastics to youngsters in surrounding towns. Now Carl owned his own gymnastic company, and he was looking for someone to travel to three small towns near Stillwater to give lessons.

"What are you doing these days?" he asked.

"I'm working at McDonald's four days a week," I said.

"Would you be interested in helping me?" Carl asked.

"Sounds fun," I said, "but unlike you, I don't have any experience in gymnastics."

"Not to worry," Carl said, "I can teach you everything you need to know."

Carl and I worked out an agreement as far as pay and hours, and the following week, he started to pick me up wherever I was staying and take me to work with him. I am pretty athletic, so it didn't take me long to learn what I needed to know to teach gymnastics. After a few months, I absolutely loved it. Working with the kids was a blast, and they always seemed to appreciate my helping them. Often when they would learn a new move, I was more excited than they were about the accomplishment. It was also great to see the parents' excitement as their children improved in their sport.

I believe a seed was planted in me during this time while working with those youngsters, a seed that would one day grow into the work I was put on this earth to do.

*****

Driving home from class one night, Carl asked me where I was living these days.

"I'm living with whoever will let me sleep on his couch," I said.

"I thought that was what you were doing," Carl said, keeping his eyes on the road.

I sank deeper into my seat, uncomfortable about where the conversation was headed or where I thought it was headed.

Prepared for a lecture, I was thus surprised when Carl told me he had already talked to his wife, Lori, about my staying in their extra bedroom, and they both thought it was a good idea.

"I'm not sure I can afford rent and utilities," I said, and as I said it, I realized how good it felt to be able to level with someone about both my finances and my living situation.

"I figured as much," Carl said. "How about if I deduct a portion of your pay to go toward bills and rent?"

It was too good a deal for me to pass up.

"I appreciate it, Carl," I said. "I'd like to take you up on your offer."

A few days later, I moved into Carl and Lori's trailer, in a trailer park on the east side of town. I didn't have to worry about any furniture because the room already had everything I needed and more—a dresser, a queen bed, a closet for the few clothes I had acquired from Kenny or others I had stayed with through the years, and even my own bathroom.

When Carl noticed how bare my closet was, he offered to loan me some money and take me shopping for some clothes at J. C. Penney. We spent a couple hundred dollars purchasing clothes and shoes, and I felt like a million bucks as I put my new clothes on hangers and hung them in my now slightly fuller closet.

For the first time in my life, I had a job, my own room, and I was paying rent. I can't begin to express how good it felt to be self-sufficient. I now know that is the place where confidence and self-esteem come from.

And it is not lost on me either that my big break came in the form of family, albeit not my immediate kin. Once again, as when I was a child, I was learning that there are people willing to help if you're willing to help yourself, and if you're willing to accept their help.

The first person I wanted to invite to my new home was Kristin.

I did just that at the first opportunity. Remembering the grand tour I gave her of my room still makes me chuckle.

"Here is my bed," I said as we stepped inside.

We walked a few more steps into the room, and I pointed at the dresser.

"Here is my dresser," I added.

I opened a few of the dresser drawers so she could see that my clothes were neatly folded. True, there weren't many clothes in the drawers; nonetheless, I was proud of what I had and how organized they were.

I led her over to the closet and showed her all eight to ten shirts hanging inside. I don't remember her saying anything as I showed off my room; I was too overcome with joy just to be able to do so.

The tour over, we went to the living room to watch TV. We sat on the couch holding hands for a few hours until Kristin said she needed to go home and study.

I walked her out to her car, and we stood and talked for a few more minutes. Buoyed by how well the visit and tour had gone, I decided it was time to come clean about where I had been living before moving in with Carl.

"Kristin, I have something to tell you," I said nervously.

She turned and looked at me. "Okay, Alton."

I took a deep breath, and then the truth just tumbled out.

"All this time you thought you were dropping me off at that apartment complex because my mom lived there. Well, my mom doesn't live there; she lives around the corner. I lied to you because I was so embarrassed at how old and run-down her house is."

Kristin smiled and said, "I know, Alton."

And then my girlfriend told me that one day after dropping me off at the apartments, she had watched me leave the complex through the parking lot and followed me to a small house, the house where my mom lived. She told me she had known for a while but hadn't said anything because I seemed to not want her to know.

"I don't care where you live, Alton. You should have just told me," she said, and with a hug, she got in her car and left.

Once again, Kristin had surprised me for the better.

Chapter 23

Meet the Parents

As Kristin and I spent more of our free hours together, I knew it was just a matter of time before I met her parents. I did not look forward to it, and I was in no hurry for that day to come.

Convinced, I had nothing going for myself, I had always been suspicious of her friends and what they thought about her dating a black guy, especially one like me with so few prospects. Most of her friends were from high school, and if any of them didn't like my dating Kristin, I never heard about it.

I also never saw Kristin give any sign that she worried about what her friends or others thought about our being together. I was the one who had the issues. I worried that her friends were talking about us behind her back. I worried what Kristin's parents would say about her dating a black guy, and a former foster kid to boot.

Kristin had admitted she was a little concerned about how her parents would react to her being in an interracial relationship, but she was also very matter-of-fact about it.

"They will probably have a problem with it in the beginning," she said, "but once they meet you, things will be okay."

Aging Out

She had more faith in her parents then I did. I was convinced they were going to hate me no matter what. And I knew Kristin was apprehensive about my meeting them, so we dated for about a year before I ever did.

The big day came the summer of 1989. Oklahoma State University was hosting the Special Olympics Summer Games. Kristin's brother, Cole, was competing in several events, and her parents were coming to town for the weekend to watch him. It was Kristin's idea to have me go with her to watch Cole's events. She had long wanted me to meet Cole, and this would allow me to also meet her parents.

"I don't think it's a good idea," I said. "I'm fine with keeping our relationship a secret a little longer."

"It'll be fine," Kristin promised. "We need to do it and get it over with."

I finally agreed. The day of the meeting, we walked onto the OSU track and spotted her parents in the bleachers a few rows from the top. I was so nervous I was already playing in my head all the ways this encounter could go bad. As we walked up the steps, I kept my head and eyes down. I did not want to make eye contact with either of her parents.

Finally, we were standing before them. Kristin gave each of them a hug, and then she turned to me and said, "Mom and Dad, this is my friend Alton."

It was obvious they had instantly connected the name with that of the fellow who was reportedly dating their daughter. If asked, I would have sworn their moods changed as that realization sank in. They both stared at me for a few seconds, and then her father, Dean, stuck out his hand and said, "Nice to meet you, Alton."

I shook his hand and replied with the same.

Kristin's mom, Cheryl, said, "Hello, Alton," and then took her seat. Kristin and I found a spot to sit on the row below her parents', I couldn't concentrate on the track and field events taking place below, so consumed was I with the awkward greeting I had just experienced.

Meanwhile, Kristin seemed just fine, and soon she was cheering the athletes on below. As for me, well, I couldn't muster the enthusiasm; I wanted nothing more than to leave, the sooner the better.

I leaned over and said to Kristin, "I told you that your parents wouldn't like me."

Kristin just gave me a pat. "It'll all be fine," she said. "There's nothing to worry about."

Thirty minutes later, Kristin finally located her brother down on the track. Cole was walking to the starting line for the fifty-yard dash. As the race began, Kristin and her parents stood and started cheering loudly for him, yelling, "Go, Cole, go!"

I stood, too, and joined them in clapping for Cole, but I was too nervous to cheer.

After the meet was over, we said our good-byes to her parents, and we walked down to the track so Kristin could introduce me to her brother.

"Hey, Cole, I want you to meet my good friend Alton."

"Hi, Alton, nice to meet you. My name is Cole Keith."

"It's nice to meet you too, Cole," I said.

Cole held up one of the medals hanging by a ribbon from his neck. "I got first place."

"I see that," I said. "You did a great job!"

"Tank you," Cole said, shortening the traditional "thank you" in his own sweet way and smiling wide.

From the moment I met Cole, I fell in love with him. All almost five feet of him is so kind, and I knew in my bones that he didn't see or care what color my skin was.

When we left the stadium that day, all I could think about was what Kristin's parents were thinking about me and what they were probably saying about me to each other. I was certain they were bothered that their daughter was dating a black guy, and I was worried that they would hate and judge me before they had a chance to get to know me. I also worried about what they would say when they learned I wasn't a college boy but an underemployed, recently homeless former foster kid.

While I fretted, Kristin seemed to set it aside. I tried the rest of the night to get her to talk about it, but she refused. I reminded her that I had said they would be upset when they found out we were dating, but she insisted they already knew.

Aging Out

I told myself Dean and Cheryl had every reason to dislike me. Heck, from the first time I had met Kristin, I believed she was too good for me.

I told her that if it came down to her having to choose between her parents or me, she needed to choose them.

"I am not worth you losing your mom and dad, Kristin."

She replied, "I won't have to choose between you and my parents, but if I did have to choose, you are worth it."

Chapter 24

Getting to Know You

Cole and I hit it off right from the start over movies, professional wrestling, and basketball. Over time, Cheryl and Dean grew fond of me as well, and I started to make the trip with Kristin to their home in Tulsa for dinner and family gatherings.

Although I never doubted Cole being happy to see me on those visits, I always wondered if Kristin and her folks ever talked about the interracial dating thing. If they did, she never told me.

I was nervous in those early days, unsure of my welcome. Spending time with Cole was easy because I never felt like I had to do anything but be myself. The same wasn't always true with the rest of Kristin's family. When we all gathered in the living room before or after dinner, Kristin's parents could go for long periods of time without addressing me personally. When I happened to be left alone with one or the other of them, the lulls in the conversation could get long. Kristin could always tell when I was on edge, and she did what she could to calm me down.

What was wrong, I realize now, had little to do with the color of my skin and much more to do with what they didn't know about me. Cheryl loves all her three kids unconditionally, and like a mama bear, she would do anything to protect them and keep them safe, including safe from wayward boyfriends.

Kristin's parents might not have had much to say to me in the beginning, but they always treated me with respect, greeting me with a welcome at the door of their home, finding me a comfortable seat in the living room, and being sure to offer me a beverage or something to eat.

I know now that Cheryl just wanted to make sure I was going to be a guy who would be nice to her daughter. I could have been plaid so long as I had the makings of a good husband and father.

With the passing of time, Dean and Cheryl and I grew closer. We grew more comfortable with each other—to the point that we would call each other on the phone from time to time just to talk.

I began to trust the man who would one day be my father-in-law when I realized he just wanted what was best for his daughter and that he would do anything to make her happy. Pretty soon, he was offering to help whenever a construction, automotive, or electrical problem came our way. The turning point in our relationship, however, came over some car wax.

The paint job on the old silver-and-blue truck I was driving by then had started to fade, and I didn't know what to do, so I called and asked Dean. He told me the name of a certain type of wax that would stop the paint from fading, but he'd no more given me the name than he said, "Just bring the truck to my house, and I'll help you wax it. I have the type of wax you need right here on the shelf in the garage."

Kristin and I headed to Tulsa, and when we arrived, Dean was standing in the driveway with the car wax in one hand and rags in the other, ready to get started. Kristin gave her dad a peck on the cheek and headed inside; I followed Dean over to my truck. I had never waxed a vehicle before, and so Dean patiently showed me the proper circular motion for putting wax on and off. We spent several hours waxing that old truck and talking about cars. When we ran out of car talk, Dean told me about his life growing up in Perry, Oklahoma, and how he was only the second person in his family to graduate from high school and the only one to graduate from college. As he shared stories of his rough childhood, I realized our youth was in many ways more alike than different. And he was 100 percent right about the car wax; my truck didn't look new, but it looked a whole lot better leaving their house than it had arriving.

If Kristin's dad and I found our common ground outside over a car, her mother and I did the same inside in the kitchen. To this day, one of my favorite things to do is help my mother-in-law cook and clean. She's one of the best cooks I know, and I enjoy helping her set the table, taking things in and out of the oven, and even washing the dishes after a big family meal. Part of the appeal, I suspect, is that she can always be heard to say, "Thank you, Alton, for your help" at the end.

In my life, there have only been a handful of people to whom I have had the courage to say, "I love you," and Cheryl is one of them.

Preconceived notions about people can make you blind to their gifts and merit.

Love can allow one to see.

Either one of Kristin's parents would come running if we needed their help with anything, big or small. They were the first family I had ever seen that did not let their personal opinions and perspectives destroy their relationships with each other. Whether or not they liked me in the beginning, they allowed Kristin to make her own decision as to whom she wanted to be with in the end.

Chapter 25

A Better Man

Being with Kristin made me want to be a better man, a man worthy of her and her love. My girlfriend was doing well at college, and I knew I needed to do something to better my life and help to ensure a happy future for us both. I wanted to give college another shot, but I could not see me surviving a semester at OSU. I had heard people talk about Langston University, a small college about twenty-five minutes south of Stillwater; the school was about the same size as Southwestern, so I thought it might be a good fit for me.

Langston University is Oklahoma's only historic black college, and it is the heart of the town of Langston, one of the more than fifty all-black towns settled by African Americans after the Civil War, the most of any state in the union. Langston remains the most successful of those all-black towns, one of the few left in the state. None of that had anything to do with why I wanted to go to school there—I'd just heard it was a small, good university, but it's a nice little piece of historic trivia about the place.

Sometime in late 1989, a friend gave me a ride to Langston University so I could check out the campus for myself. On that same trip, I stopped by the registrar's office to learn what it would take for me to get enrolled and the financial aid office to see what was available because I had no money for tuition or books.

Back in Stillwater, I spent the next few days trying to figure out what I should do and if I could do it. I wanted to go back to school, but I had no car and so no way to get back and forth to Langston for classes. I had no money, so I had no way to pay for gas even if I could find someone to take me.

I was quickly talking myself out of returning to college. It was Kristin who insisted that going back to school was the smart thing to do and I could get financial aid to do so.

"And if you need a ride," she told me, "I'll drive you."

Other than being scared, I suddenly had no good excuse not to return to college.

Leaving Southwestern as I had did not make it easy for me to return. Because I had left without withdrawing from school, I had no idea how to access those records. Instead, Kristin suggested I call Cushing High School and ask to have my transcript and ACT scores sent to Langston's admission office. Meanwhile, Kristin and I spent several hours filling out the forms in the financial-aid packet.

A few weeks later, I received an acceptance letter from LU. I was officially a college student again.

No sooner had I been accepted than the fear and anxiety set in. I felt just as I had in Kansas, and my worries were the same as well: I was afraid I wouldn't be able to find my classes. I worried I would not be smart enough to do the work. And I feared to my very core that I would not be able to even read the textbooks or the notes the professors put on the board.

The idea of facing the first day of class was enough to make me tear that acceptance letter up and pretend it had never arrived.

But I didn't, and in refraining, I took another step toward the life of my dreams.

There was no only the simple question of how to get me to Langston. Kristin had offered to take me whenever she could from the get-go, but she couldn't do it every day—thankfully, when we got my schedule, my classes were all on Tuesdays and Thursdays that first semester. I would only have to find a ride to and from class twice a week.

Kristin and I made the commute work by having her take me early in the morning to Langston so she could get back to Stillwater in time for her own commitments. We'd do the same for the return trip. After all those years of hanging out waiting for a ride to the Annex or Kristin's dorm, I knew how to kill time until someone could give me a lift.

The first day of school arrived, and my very first class was American history, taught by a professor from Africa who spoke broken English. I found him difficult to understand, and I sat in the back of the packed classroom—hoping no one would notice I was older than everyone else. This made hearing more difficult, which proved unexpectedly beneficial, because that's how I met Chris.

Chris was a single mom of two girls who, like me, was returning to school in hopes of getting her bachelor's degree. Our first words to each other were about how we both felt like we didn't belong there because we were so much older than our fellow freshmen classmates. By the time class was over, we had also determined that we both lived in Stillwater and would be commuting to Langston.

At the end of class, Chris asked, "Would you mind carpooling with me? I'm making the trip five days a week."

"I'd be happy to help with the driving," I said, "but I don't have a car, and I only have class on Tuesdays and Thursdays."

"It'd be great not to have to make the drive alone every day, so if you want to ride with me two days a week, that'd be fine."

I would have liked to have been able to offer Chris some money for gas, but I didn't have any money to give her. I only hoped my company and conversation on the road would be payment enough. They must have been because for the next two semesters I made the round-trip from Stillwater to Langston with Chris until I got tired of the commute and all the time school took and dropped out at the end of my second semester.

Chapter 26

The Power of Knowing

I had not managed to graduate from Langston, but I did learn a few very important things about myself before I left:

    1. I could do the work.

    2. I was dyslexic.

I learned the latter after flunking a few classes at Langston. My adviser cared enough to get involved, and she had some testing done in hopes of helping me become a better student.

A diagnosis of dyslexia was the result.

It wasn't good news.

The diagnosis all but guaranteed I would always read slower and struggle with reading comprehension, but at least I finally knew my struggles in school all those years stemmed not from a lack of smarts. I had always tried my best and had always come up short.

Now I knew why. My brain flips letters so that a "b" looks like a "d," and it can be more problematic if a word contains a letter that repeats, as in the word *remember*. When I see *remember*, I see *rem-memmeber*, not *remember*.

My eyes also have a tendency to pull words from one sentence and put them in places where they shouldn't be. No one had figured this out in grade school, middle school, high school—or my first try at college. Instead, I had been put in remedial classes because first, my records told my primary and secondary educators I did not do well in English or history or science, and then second, my transcript told Southwestern and Langston the same thing. My poor performance in school became kind of a self-fulfilling prophecy.

In fact, because of my dyslexia, I have become more of an auditory learner—I learn better by listening than from what I see or read. If my dyslexia had been diagnosed earlier, chances are arrangements could have been made that would have improved my performance at school as a kid or in how I took the ACT, which would have probably meant better grades and better scores.

As relieved as I was to finally know what had been holding me back in school, I was also embarrassed. Embarrassed because I didn't want any special treatment because of my problem. Embarrassed because I didn't want to be labeled as someone with a disability.

Misplaced pride and ignorance were my downfall this time.

I didn't tell a soul about my diagnosis when I got it because it sounded bad to me. I wanted nothing to do with it. It would be years before I was comfortable enough in my own skin that I could admit I had a learning disability; before I could ask for or accept help; before I could let someone proof my papers for college or double-check something written for work.

I left Langston with that secret.

And I carried it with me for years to come.

Chapter 27

The Proposal

After years of dating, talk turned to getting married. I think I brought it up more than Kristin did just so I could see her reaction to the idea. It must have been encouraging because after several conversations, I went to a local jewelry store and bought the only ring in the place I could afford; it cost about three hundred dollars if, memory serves.

By that time, I had seen enough movies and heard enough stories to know about the importance of being romantic when popping the big question. I wanted to do that for Kristin, but not with the ring I had.

I was scared that she would get so excited about seeing me down on one knee with the ring box holding the engagement ring of her dreams in my hand that the disappointment of seeing the ring inside would cause her to run away crying in disappointment.

Once again, my insecurities, my inner fears, robbed someone else of a special moment. And looking back, I know now the scenario I concocted was an insult to Kristin, who has always had her values in the right place.

Aging Out

Kristin never got the romantic proposal she so deserved and I so wanted her to have. Instead, after carrying the ring around for several days, I just handed it to her while we were watching TV and said, "We can get married now."

She didn't say a word, just took the box, opened it, and put the ring on her finger. I know she wasn't thrilled about my proposal, but she never complained about the ring and always wore it with pride.

A few days after my poor excuse of a proposal, I apologized for the ring not being what I thought Kristin had hoped it would be. She just shook her head.

"I don't care how much the ring cost," she said. "It's not about the ring. I just wanted to spend the rest of my life with you, Alton."

Soon after that, Kristin was invited to a wedding of one of her high school friends, and she told me her parents would be going as well.

"You should come too, so we can tell them we're engaged," she said.

"Well, I'll go, but I don't know about telling your parents yet," I said.

"I'll do the telling," said Kristin. "You just need to be there."

We met Kristin's parents and Cole at the church, and I prayed throughout the entire ceremony that Kristin's mom would spot the ring on her daughter's left hand, and the gig would be up. Kristin's surprise would be ruined, yes, but I would be absolved for having failed to ask Dean for her hand in marriage.

Luck was not with me that day. Neither of Kristin's parents spotted the ring during the wedding, but when we met them afterward for dinner at a local restaurant, Cole spotted it right away.

"My sister's getting married!" he yelled, before we could say a thing.

Kristin's face turned bright red. Cheryl sat silent in what I can only surmise was shock before she asked to see the ring. The room fell silent for what was probably only a few seconds at most, but it felt like an eternity to me. I don't recall any comments about the ring from her mother or father, but they congratulated us both on our engagement, and we proceeded to order and eat. I had no idea how to lighten the mood, so I sat in silence while Kristin explained that we planned to marry in August of 1995.

After we had finished the meal and said our good-byes, we all got into our respective cars and headed home. Neither Kristin nor I was sure as to what her parents' true feelings were about the news. I was afraid they'd been so quiet at dinner simply because they didn't want to cause a scene in a public place. I was convinced they were disappointed with the ring and thought Kristin shouldn't marry me if I couldn't afford better. Looking back, I was the one whose priorities were out of whack. Marriage isn't about the size of the diamond but your readiness to love and care for another. I suspect that was what Dean and Cheryl were wondering about.

Kristin didn't say much on the way home either, but it was obvious it all bothered me more than it did her. I had wanted her parents' blessing—even though I had not been man enough to go to her father and ask him for her hand.

To their credit, her folks did not seem to hold that against me. When it came time to plan the wedding, Kristin's parents were right there helping us ensure it would be one to remember.

Chapter 28

Married Life

Kristin and I were married on August 12, 1995, at Sunnybrook Christian Church in Stillwater, Oklahoma, with John Tally performing the wedding. My best man was my grandpa, and the groomsmen were Michael Davis, Mitch Carson, and Blaine Douglas—all men I had become good friends with over the years. Kristin's maid of honor was her sister, Kelly, and the bridesmaids were two of her high school friends, Lisa and Sherri.

We went to San Antonio, Texas, for our honeymoon, but after a few days, we decided to return home to Stillwater. We would use the money we saved from our honeymoon budget to buy a couch and another piece of furniture for our little house. I also called my job and told them I would be coming back early.

From day one, I was scared of being married. I just knew I would come home someday and Kristin would be gone—or worse, she'd be there, waiting to tell me she no longer wanted to be my wife and was leaving me.

Truth be told, I always thought she had married me because she was such a kind person and she felt sorry for me. I worried that she

would come to her senses and want nothing to do with me. If she had run for the hills in those first months after we wed, I would have understood.

I spent most of my time sifting through my childhood, trying—in spite of it—to make rational decisions, reasonable, grown-up decisions, the kind a woman would want a husband to make or help with. Unfortunately, as a child, I had never seen such things modeled by the adults in my family.

And I carried some unusual quirks into our marriage: First, I was thrilled to have a refrigerator, a working refrigerator—not a possession that gets that many guys very excited. I was also mesmerized by the reality of having edible food, no matter how little, in that refrigerator.

What I mean is, I would find myself getting up in the middle of the night and going into the kitchen where I would open the refrigerator and spend a few minutes looking at what little food was inside.

Kristin saw me do this one time and before I could say anything, she knew what I was doing. She told me I was looking in the refrigerator because I had never had food to eat when I was a child, and now that I was an adult, I felt the urge to check to make sure the food that had been there at the end of the day still existed.

She was absolutely right. Yet despite knowing that, I found it hard to stop myself from checking the refrigerator every now and then.

*****

I had always known Kristin had a good heart and a good head on her shoulders, and that only became more evident after our marriage. Whether it was cutting the honeymoon short because the money could be better spent on a necessity or opening our home to others in need, Kristin never hesitated or complained.

We were soon keeping my cousin Martina's two boys as often as we could because they were being left at my grandparents' house just like my siblings, their mom, and I used to be as children—only Grandma and Grandpa were now almost fifteen years older.

Aging Out

Kristin was a trooper and treated the boys as if they were her own kids. We spent what little extra money we had on buying them clothes and the stuff of childhood: little toys, picture books, candy.

I wanted to be for those boys what no one, save maybe my grandpa, ever was for me: the person they could count on in all situations. In that spirit, I tried to be there when they needed me—no matter what. We loved those boys and would have given anything to have them as our own.

The same went for my sister and her kids. Kristin and I spent a lot of time babysitting Kesha's children. My sister had become more like my mom than she cared to admit. She'd ask us to keep her kids while she went out on the town, and then, just like Mom, she rarely returned when she said she would. Sometimes it would be days before she came to pick the children up.

We were happy to have the children stay with us, but it upset me that Kesha was doing to her children exactly what had been done to us as kids. I remember what it felt like when Mom would drop us off at my grandparents'. I loved my grandparents, but I wanted to be with my mom. There was always a hole in my heart when she left, one that didn't get filled until her return.

I can remember as if it was yesterday Mom dropping us off at Grandma's, telling all of us she would be back later that night, only to be disappointed over and over again when she didn't show up that evening or the next morning or the day after that.

I kept thinking if Kesha would only remember what that had felt like, maybe it would stop her from doing the same thing to her children.

And if she didn't remember, I was sure to remind her every chance I got.

For the most part, we kept my sister's children voluntarily, although there were times when she got in trouble with the Department of Human Services, and one or two of the children would be removed from her home temporarily.

Yet no matter how bad things were, no matter what it was she had done, my sister always somehow got her kids back. Kristin and I would have gladly taken them in, only I knew that would cause an all-out war with my sister, and the rest of my family would have hated me for stepping in.

So instead, we kept the kids whenever Kesha needed, and I took advantage of every opportunity to remind my sister about the importance of putting one's children first.

I would have thought she never heard me except that when Kesha got mad at me, the first thing she'd do was tell me I could not see her kids anymore. It was another echo from the past. When Mom used to get mad at our grandparents for suggesting she stay home more or clean up her act, Mom's response was to tell them to stay away from us. I remember Grandma calling DHS and filing a report because she was mad at my mom. Later, when Grandma had custody of us and they had a fight, Mom would file her own report with DHS.

I didn't understand this at all. As a child, I asked them both why they called the police when they were only mad at each other. I tried to explain to them that using DHS to get back at each other was only hurting all of us, the very children they said they cared about.

Chapter 29

Chasing Dreams

In our first years together, I did everything I knew to do to provide for Kristin—always chasing dreams in hopes of being able to give her a comfortable life. I switched jobs all the time, always with the hope that the new job would be the one that would make me feel like a good provider. But without a college degree, that good job proved elusive.

In 1994, the year before we married, I brought in $11,600—the poverty threshold for a couple our age was $10,259.

The lack of a well-paying job meant I often had to work more than one job. For several years, I worked as an instructor at out-of-town cheerleading camps during the summers. It didn't pay much, and I should have given it up sooner. My reluctance to do so was rooted in my belief that if only I worked hard enough, I would someday get promoted and make the big bucks—well, if not the big bucks at least more than $5.50 an hour.

That job not only put us on hard times financially, it also kept me away from home for weeks at a time. My intentions were good but my judgment was terrible, and I refused to listen to Kristin when she told me that I needed to find a steady job, ideally one with benefits such as health care, sick leave, and paid vacation.

I did eventually find steady employment with benefits at Stillwater Middle School and worked there for several years, but once again, the pay was barely enough for us to make ends meet. By 1999, I was bringing home $23,715 a year, and we had a baby, with another on the way. The U. S. poverty threshold in 2000 for a family of four was $17,603—and the average income in Oklahoma, one of the lowest in the country, was more than $32,000. No wonder we were always playing catch-up.

Still, I remember working at the middle school as a wonderful job because I got to spend my whole day with youngsters.

My official title was office assistant, but I spent very little time in the office. I was usually to be found supervising the playground during lunch or walking the halls when classes changed. I kept track of tardy slips and escorted kids who got in trouble to the office.

I loved working there and learned a lot about myself while working with those students. Kristin would say it was where I got a glimpse of the kind of work I was born to do.

I encountered so much that would eventually help me grow as a person. I saw too many abused and neglected youngsters. Like me, they didn't dare share what was going on at home, but I could tell; I saw me in them. Just as I had, they acted out in class and were disrespectful to adults—cries for help that too often went unrecognized by the adults around them.

I did my best to try to read between the lines, and my heart cried out for them. I wanted to help them because I knew what they were going through. I wanted to help the teachers, administrators, and staff to understand the bricks these children carried to school every day, but I just didn't know how.

Dreams aren't always about the money, about the lack of it or the getting of it.

Sometimes dreams are about more important stuff, like what you want to do with your time on this earth.

*****

Aging Out

Eventually, I became friends with a sixth-grade science teacher named Jacob Ehrlich, who had an amazing amount of patience when it came to those students whom other teachers had labeled as being "troubled kids."

Jacob had a way of making any child feel seen and important. Of all the students he helped, none posed more of a challenge than a young boy named Tim, a kid who had exasperated every teacher in the school save for his science teacher.

Hidden behind too big clothes and long, uncombed hair, Tim did not appear to have many friends. He was always more likely to be seen sitting by himself, than with others. It wasn't that he was shy. Tim would talk to anyone who would listen. It was just that no one—not his fellow students nor his teachers—wanted to hear what he had to say. The impression I got was that he just seemed to bug or annoy young and old alike. He wasn't a kid who got in fights, nor was he disrespectful. No, when it came to the classroom, his issues were that he struggled to pay attention or to sit still, and he rarely did his classwork—much less his homework.

And then one day I learned that Tim was failing all of his classes except Jacob's science class, and I was curious as to why. I promised myself I would ask Jacob the next chance I got. A few days later, the opportunity arose just before the bell that signaled the start of the day.

"Hey, Jacob, I hear you have Tim in your class. What's your take on him?"

Jacob didn't even hesitate.

"Tim is misunderstood," he said.

"What do you mean by that?" I asked.

"Come by my classroom during third hour, and you'll see what I mean," he said, mysteriously.

When third hour rolled around, I was sitting in the back of Jacob's science class. At first, I didn't notice anything special. Jacob took roll and began his class with a lecture.

A few minutes into the lecture, Tim got up and starting walking around the classroom, looking at the posters on the walls, and talking to himself under his breath. All the other students remained seated.

And just when I was about to tell Tim to sit down, Jacob asked the class a question about what he had just presented in his lecture.

And Tim answered it.

And Jacob asked another question.

And Tim answered it.

And so it went, over and over again. Without hesitation, the boy who was out of his seat answered almost every question while he continued to circle the room. I was amazed that Jacob had taken the time to figure this out about a boy everyone else had written off.

*****

One of my first attempts to help kids outside of my own family also came about thanks to Jacob. I helped him start a Fellowship of Christian Athletes chapter at the middle school. We met in the library every Friday morning before school for a devotion and prayer.

The group started off small, but in just a few months, it had grown to three hundred students.

The only downside of all this was that I was still struggling with my own faith. I wasn't even sure I was a Christian. What I did know was that I wanted to help Jacob help as many students as we possibly could, so when I became an FCA leader, I did my best to hide any doubts I had when it came to my beliefs.

I led devotions and prayed with the students, all the while wondering about my own soul. It wasn't because I didn't know what it took to be a Christian, but because of the conditions and conflicting environment in which I had learned about God and Christianity, it was difficult to believe I was part of God's plan.

Still carrying my own bricks, what did I have that could help anyone else?

It was at about that time that I began to notice this one particular middle-school girl who, like Tim, appeared to sit by herself almost every day during lunch. If my antennae were right, it wasn't that she couldn't fit in but rather that she hated herself so much she didn't even try. She reminded me of myself at that age, and I shivered at the memory of how alone I had so often felt back then. Unfortunately, at that stage in my life, I had yet to learn what I could do or say to her that would help or make a difference. I had yet to heal myself.

But one day, after seeing her eating lunch alone again and looking forlorn, I wrote this poem.

I Want to Ask You
Are things better?
Did the pain go away?
Does tomorrow tell a story?
Is the hate here to stay?
Have you fixed what is broken?
Will your tears ever run dry?
Can you forget about the past?
Does remembering make you cry?
Can words silence the storm?
Will the whispers stop the rain?
Who can keep your secrets?
Does your expression show your pain?

At the time, I thought I was writing the poem about and for the lonely lunch girl, but in hindsight, I know now it was more about me than her. Seeing her hurt forced me to recognize that I was still hurting. Writing the poem was not only an acknowledgment of that but also my first attempt to do something about it.

And then I did something else—for someone else.

I shared my poem with the lonely lunch girl. A bit fearful, afraid of looking foolish, I did so in hopes that the lonely lunch girl would realize that there was at least one other person in the world who saw her. She was not alone.

I don't recall her reaction when I gave her the poem.

I only know that later that day she came up to me and said, "I never knew anyone was paying attention."

Then she turned and walked away.

I can't say my efforts came to much, but I am glad that I did what I could and tried. The middle school was full of hurting kids who needed so much for someone to show they saw them, that they were not invisible.

In so many cases, teachers are the only constant, good things in a child's life. I was not a teacher, but I saw the value of being there when a kid needed someone. I believed that if I did my best to be available, I just might give at least one child who needed it a little hope.

And if it was only one, that would be enough for me.

Working at the middle school, I eventually came to know like I know my name that kids don't want or need perfect people. They just want someone to care enough to notice them and accept them for who they are. They want real people who have struggles just like they do. They want teachers and parents who have the courage to take ownership of their mistakes.

And what they need is to see forgiveness in its purest form, over and over again.

They need to witness the journey of healing so they can then repeat the process in their own lives.

And the teachers, counselors, and other adults in their lives need to learn to be patient, to understand why a child who looks like she is bursting to talk, refuses to do so.

They need to realize that many children—the ones who most need a friend, a Good Samaritan, someone to talk to—are silent because they have been taught all their lives by their parents, just like I was, never, ever, ever to tell.

Chapter 30

Random Acts

I had a routine at the middle school when I walked the halls. I always started on the second floor and worked my way down the main hall, checking the bathrooms, nooks, and crannies where kids could hide and skip class before walking the side halls.

On one particular day, I was headed down the main hall when I saw a boy with his head down slouched in a desk outside the counselor's office. I squinted to see if it was anyone I recognized, but to no avail. About ten yards away, I finally realized it was a boy named Johnny. I took in all I could from his body language before I pulled even with him.

"Hey, Johnny, what are you doing?"

Johnny didn't move or answer. In fact, he completely ignored me. I knew he had heard me the first time, but nonetheless, I came a little closer and said again, "Johnny, why are you sitting out here in the hall?" Again, Johnny kept his head down, staring at the top of the desk with a single-minded focus I had to admire.

The third time I spoke, I was standing only a few feet from him, and I bent down, hoping that by doing so my presence would force him to take his eyes off the desk and look at me. I said again, "Johnny what's wrong?"

Johnny lifted his head and looked me in the eye.

"Nothing, Alton."

With that, his head dropped back to its original position.

It was obvious that nothing was, indeed, something but equally obvious that Johnny wasn't going to share.

I didn't take it personally. Instead, I stood up, reached in my pocket, pulled out a Jolly Rancher, and set it on the desk in front of him. And then I turned and continued down the hall.

I looked back only once, after I had reached the end of the hall and turned the corner, positioning myself so Johnny couldn't see me. In a flash almost too quick to see, I saw Johnny grab the piece of candy and with a pull and a twist, open it and pop the Jolly Rancher into his mouth. He then placed the wrapper on the desk as a tiny smile appeared on his face.

The next day, I ran into the counselor and asked if she could tell me why Johnny had been sitting outside her office.

"He was taking a test," she said, "and his teacher noticed his ear was bleeding. She took him to the nurse's office, and Johnny told them his dad had punched him on that side of the head on his way to school."

Johnny had been sitting in the hall waiting for a DHS worker to come and get him.

Her words made me heartsick.

I had learned something, though. I harbored no delusion that one piece of candy had made all of Johnny's problems disappear that day; he was too old for that. I knew only that a kind gesture in a difficult time had eased his pain, if only for the moment it took for Johnny to open and eat a Jolly Rancher and smile.

Such small gestures of kindness by people had many a time kept me afloat as a child and as a teen, sometimes the only thing that helped me get to the next day.

Going forward, I would be on the lookout for other Johnnys that crossed my path.

Chapter 31

Grandpa

Some people get to be adults before seeing someone they love become gravely ill or die. I had not been so lucky. I was just a boy when my little brother died while I was living away from home, and I was just a young man when my grandpa was diagnosed with a brain tumor.

I can still recall hearing a siren in the distance that day, and for some reason, it seemed to call out to me. When I could hear it no longer, the sound was replaced by a queasy feeling that I couldn't shake.

The phone call came next.

"Your grandpa is in the emergency room," Grandma said.

I ran from the house to the car and drove across town to the emergency room to be with my family. I found my grandma crying, with Aunt Faye and my mom on each side of her like bookends.

"What happened?" I asked.

Grandma stopped crying long enough to tell me that after mowing the lawn, my grandpa had passed out in their bedroom. Unable to wake him, she had dialed 9-1-1.

We took turns assuring Grandma that he would be okay, although I think we were all in shock. Grandpa was our family's rock. Having him collapse was like having Gibraltar tumble into the Mediterranean Sea. He had to get better, I told myself.

After about an hour, the doctor came out, and the news was not good: Grandpa had a tumor on his brain.

The diagnosis was more than Grandma could stand, and she and my mother and aunt began to cry as they huddled together.

"What does that mean?" I asked.

He explained that the tumor was what had caused Grandpa to collapse, but he had yet to determine if it was cancerous. That would require a biopsy.

They admitted Grandpa into the hospital, and we continued to wait while the tests were run. A few hours later, a nurse came to the waiting room and announced that we could go see Grandpa, who was now resting comfortably in his own room.

The reality of his situation hit me as soon as I stepped into his room. Grandpa was unconscious; wires and tubes ran from his nose and arms. As soon as my grandma, aunt, and mother sat down, I bolted from the room, so overwhelmed with sadness that all I knew to do was run.

In my car, I cried until I didn't have the strength to cry anymore. The greatest man I knew was sick, and I was not sure if he was going to live. I felt helpless because there was nothing I could do to help him.

After several hours, I drove home to tell Kristin what had happened. She immediately returned with me to the hospital. By then, several other family members had arrived and were gathered in Grandpa's room, and to my surprise, Grandpa was awake.

Kristin and I found a spot in the corner of the hospital room and watched as my relatives took turns having a word with Grandpa.

Listening to them, I could tell something was wrong. Most of the time Grandpa just stared at whoever was talking. When he did respond or join in one of the conversations swirling around him, he spoke off topic. I wondered if I would ever again see my grandpa rigging up mowers, telling corny jokes, or sharing his own brand of life's wisdom. In the end, the tumor was, indeed, cancer. His condition was terminal, and the doctors gave him a year or so to live with treatment.

The doctor's verdict left Grandma in denial and me a wreck. Until that moment, all science to the contrary, I had believed my grandpa would live forever.

The thought of his dying had never crossed my mind.

The doctor went on to say they would help Grandma set up the treatments that would prolong his life, but she would have to take Grandpa to Oklahoma City for them. Without hesitation, Grandma accepted the help, and the doctor left the room to start making arrangements. When the doctor left the room, so did a part of my grandma. There was no doubt she was a strong and tough woman, but I had never seen this side of her before. I thought the news that Grandpa was dying would be more than she could handle, and I was worried that she would fall apart and, in doing so, so would the rest of the family.

But I was wrong.

Grandma became the strength everyone else would rely on in the days to come. I had always known my grandparents loved each other, but seeing my grandma step up to take care of Grandpa the way she did showed me how deep that love was. She sold the house and moved into a small apartment behind Braum's so she could be by my grandpa's side twenty-four hours a day.

The only time she asked for help was when Grandpa needed a ride to get to Oklahoma City for his treatment. I considered it an honor to be able to help when she called.

Chapter 32

The Good Lie

The first trip to the treatment center in Oklahoma City was hard on everyone. Grandpa would never have said it, but I saw the fear in his eyes as we entered the place. I wanted to be strong for him, but I didn't know what to say that would make a difference. So we just sat there in silence and waited for his name to be called.

When it was Grandpa's turn, the doctor explained the procedure, which involved securing a brace on my grandpa's head with four screws to keep his head from moving while they beamed radiation into the tumor. The procedure was expected to take a little more than an hour, and Grandpa would be sedated when he came out.

With each word the doctor had uttered, Grandma had become more restless. At this point, she began to cry. The doctor placed his hand on her shoulder, looked her straight in the eye, and said, "I will take care of your husband."

With that, he turned and disappeared down the hallway.

Again, Kristin, Mom, and I just sat there not knowing what to say this time that would make Grandma feel any better. A few minutes went by in silence, when all of a sudden Grandma started to tell stories about some of the funny things that had happened between her and Grandpa through the years. The one that got the whole waiting room laughing was the time she went on a business trip to Texas with Grandpa but didn't realize until they arrived that she had forgotten her false teeth. Grandpa was so mad he wouldn't even speak to her most of the trip, even after she had him call and ask Uncle Stevie to mail the teeth to Texas.

By the end of that story, I think we had all forgotten where we were, but we were jerked back to reality when the nurse came running into the waiting room saying they needed Grandma. Before anyone could ask why, Grandma was following the nurse down the hall, leaving all of us to wonder what was wrong now.

The next time we saw Grandma, she was crying, and she walked straight to me and said, "Alton you have to go help the nurse—Grandpa is trying to leave the hospital!"

I found the nurse, who showed me to the elevator and told me Grandpa had stopped the procedure under the guise of needing to go to the restroom but instead had taken off running down the hall with the IV port still in his arm.

"We tried to talk him into coming back," the nurse said, "but he refused, becoming more agitated each time we asked."

She said they had tried to corner him, but he would not let anyone near him. At that moment, the elevator door opened, and as I stepped into the hallway, I saw my grandpa in a blue hospital gown, the brace still screwed into his head, running toward an exit sign. I had never seen my grandpa act like this, and I had no idea what I was supposed to do to fix the situation.

Having failed to notice a security guard near the exit, Grandpa was now trying to retrace his steps; he finally backed himself into a corner. The sound of him yelling in fright—"Get away from me! You are not doctors, and you're running experiments on me!"—made me want to cry. It also became clear that I was the one who would have to do something to end the confrontation. The doctor handed me the syringe and told me to inject its contents directly into the IV port on Grandpa's right hand. I nodded and started to walk toward my frightened grandfather, talking to him in a soft, low voice.

"Tell me what's wrong, Grandpa," I said.

"Alton, they are running experiments on me, and I am not going to let them do it anymore."

"That's not what they are doing. Grandpa, you are in the doctor's office getting treatment for your tumor."

He insisted I didn't understand and pleaded, "Alton, you need to believe me."

I wanted to believe him because I had never seen my grandpa act like this before. As I got closer, I noticed blood running down his head from the screw holes. I also heard the doctor at the far end of the hall yelling, "Alton, see if you can get him into one of the rooms!"

I was now close enough to Grandpa that I could touch him, so I put my hand on his shoulder and asked him to go into the closest room with me. He looked me in the eyes.

"I'll go in the room as long as you lock the door and don't let anyone else in."

I agreed, and together we walked into the examination room. I also did as I had promised and locked the door behind us. With the door locked, he began to complain again about seeing strange lights and needing to let the government know about the experiments going on there.

Before I could respond, the doctor came to the door and asked me to step out into the hall. At the sight of him, Grandpa started screaming, "Get away from me!"

I moved to the door, and then told my grandpa I was going to step out of the room for just a moment to tell the doctor to leave.

Reluctantly, Grandpa let me step out, but only after I had promised I would get him out of the hospital on my return. It was a lie, but a necessary one this time. I had to promise him so he would calm down.

Outside in the hall, the doctor stressed the urgency of my getting the syringe into the IV so its contents could calm Grandpa down.

"What's wrong with him?" I whispered.

"The tumor in his brain is causing him to be paranoid and hallucinate," he explained.

It all made sense. I told the doctor to please stay out of sight, and

I'd get the medicine into Grandpa's IV as fast as I could.

Back in the room, I locked the door.

"What did the doctor say?" Grandpa asked.

"He said I need to give you a shot in your IV to calm you down," I told him. "Once I give you that, we can leave."

I walked over to Grandpa and took his arm; he didn't resist. As I inserted the syringe into the IV, he looked up at me and asked, "Alton, why are you doing this to me? You don't understand what they were doing to me in there."

His eyes were filled with hurt, and he looked so disappointed in me. It recalled the day he had learned I had dropped out of college. I had thought that was the worst I could ever feel.

I was wrong. This was much worse.

This time my betrayal was more than he could handle, and when I gave him the shot, there was nothing left in him. With a look of defeat on his face, he drifted off to sleep.

I loved my grandpa more than life itself, and I knew giving him the medicine that day was the right thing to do, but it hurt like hell to do it.

I unlocked the door and stepped outside. I asked the doctor what was going to happen to Grandpa now. He said there would be no more treatments that day; they were going to take the halo off his head, and the nurses would get him back to his room so he could rest.

The doctor escorted me back to the waiting room. I could only imagine what everyone had been thinking since I'd left. The doctor told Grandma I'd been brave, and she should be proud of me. And then he explained Grandpa was done for the day, and we could take him home in a few hours.

The ride home was unnaturally quiet because no one knew what to say. I could see hurt and embarrassment in Grandpa's eyes, and we all hurt for him.

The only words spoken came at the end, and they came from my grandpa.

"I'm not going back to that treatment facility again."

Chapter 33

We're Pregnant!

A few months after Grandpa was diagnosed with the brain tumor, we learned Kristin was pregnant. Life has a funny way of balancing out the bad with the good like that.

I was equally excited and scared about the baby news. While my dreams of becoming a father looked to be coming true, in the back of my mind was a little voice spewing doubt that threatened to cripple me.

I wanted to be a good dad. I just had no idea what I was supposed to do to be a good dad. The little voice in my head told me over and over that I was going to fail no matter how hard I tried, no matter what I did, no matter what I didn't do.

Bottom line: I didn't know how to be a dad. How could I? I'd never even met my own. Heck, I didn't even know his name.

The only man who had shown me even a glimpse of what a man or father should be was slowly fading away from the tumor that was consuming his brain. Several times a week, I would go by and visit my grandparents. Grandma was working around the clock to make sure Grandpa was comfortable. Most of my visits entailed sitting beside his bed and catching him up on the news as he faded in and out of consciousness.

During every one of my visits, I would remind Grandpa that Kristin was pregnant and that the baby's middle name was going to be Thomas.

"After you, Grandpa," I said.

I knew he was dying, and I had accepted it. I just wanted him to live long enough to see his grandson and hold him in his arms, and I prayed and pleaded with God to allow that.

Occasionally on one of my visits, Grandpa would be alert and talkative, which usually meant his pain medicine had worn off. This was a double-edged sword. It left him more aware of his surroundings but also of the pain he was in. I'll never forget the last conversation we had on just such a day.

"Alton, I have something for you," he said in a hoarse whisper. He took his arm and moved it until his hand was resting on the nightstand beside his bed. He shook his hand back and forth moving papers around until an envelope became visible. He pinched the envelope between two fingers and slowly moved his arm toward me and said, "Here."

I took the envelope and asked him what was inside.

"Open it," he said.

I did as he instructed and reached inside. I pulled out a single dollar bill. I looked at him questioningly.

"What's this, Grandpa? Why are you giving me a dollar?"

"I am giving you back the dollar bill you gave me years ago."

I looked at him quite puzzled, and then I remembered. He was saying this was the same dollar bill I had given him for Christmas back when I was living at the boys ranch, the Christmas when I returned home with presents for everyone paid for by myself, the Christmas when I received not a single gift from my family.

I held the bill tight. I had thought my gift meant little or nothing to him, and now I knew it had meant enough for him to hold onto it for almost twenty years. With tears rolling down my face, I leaned over, hugged him, and told him I loved him. That would be the last time I spoke with my grandpa, and that embrace would be our last. He slipped away a few days later. I was in Texas, working at a cheerleading camp, when he died. Kristin called to tell me and to let me know my family would wait until the end of the week to have the funeral. It was such a relief; I would be back in Oklahoma by then and able to say my final good-bye to the man who had been my only hero as a boy.

A few days later, Kristin called again: My family had decided to hold the funeral the next morning.

I was devastated and angry; I had ridden to Texas with someone else—I had no way to get home to Stillwater in time. Part of me was also justifiably hurt that my family would go ahead with Grandpa's funeral without me; the other part was used to such slights. I feared I would always be to most of my family the worthless kid who sent Uncle Stevie to jail.

At camp the following morning, I had a hard time teaching cheers and paying attention. I could feel my heart filling with hatred and resentment because I was not at the funeral, although I was thankful Kristin would be. I'm sad to say I allowed those negative feelings to fester inside me for many years, much longer than I should have.

When I returned home, Kristin told me the service had been beautiful and lots of people had come to pay their respects. I should have been grateful for that. I should have been grateful that I got to hug him and tell him I loved him before he passed.

Instead, I was bitter and feeling sorry for myself. It took me some time to understand why I was so hurt. And then it all made a little more sense.

Being left out of Grandpa's funeral recalled all the hurt I had felt as a boy at learning of my little brother Watell's death from an asthma attack in a phone call days after he died, hurt compounded by not being brought home from the boys ranch to attend his funeral.

These two deaths were years apart, as were the slights that accompanied them, but together, the pain I felt in their aftermath threatened to consume me—another brick that I chose to carry.

Chapter 34

Fatherhood

For the most part, Kristin had a normal pregnancy; my behavior, however, was not. Some of what I did was typical of a first-time father-to-be: I read every book I could on having a baby. I went with Kristin to every doctor's appointment and bought a stethoscope to listen to the baby's heartbeat. I rubbed Kristin's swollen feet and made her nutritious breakfasts.

But I also was so into her pregnancy that I shared personal matters with others that intruded on my wife's privacy. And if she dared skip her prenatal vitamins because they were making her morning sickness worse, I got mad and lectured her about what that could do to the baby.

I didn't go so far as to gain sympathy weight, but I did go overboard telling people what I was doing for Kristin and the pregnancy, and constantly asking questions of everyone, so much so that you'd have thought I was the one who was pregnant.

My heart was in the right place. I wanted to be the world's greatest dad, but I should probably have been focused first on being a great husband to the woman who was pregnant.

I know now that I wanted to look to the world—our friends, her family, people on the street—like I knew what I was doing because I needed people to look at me and see that I was going to be a great dad.

I think I thought if I could see that in the faces of friends, family, and even strangers, I might start to believe it myself.

On the surface, I suspect I did look like I had it together, at least as well as most new fathers. But what did I know about being a husband, much less a father? Absolutely nothing. But I sure acted like I did. Maybe I would have been better off reading books about being a husband and a father instead of *What To Expect When You're Expecting*. Reading such books, however, would have exposed my insecurities as a man, and I certainly did not want the world to know that I had no idea what I was doing as a husband, much less as someone about to become a dad.

I loved Kristin more than anything, but I didn't love myself, and that kept me from being a good husband. If only I had known that to be a good dad I had to first be a good husband, and to be a good husband, I needed to be a friend.

I needed my wife to help me find my way but at first refused to let her. When my heart cried out for help, she heard it and tried to respond, but my past chased away any advice she gave me. Instead, I did the only thing I knew to do. I pretended to know what I was doing until I figured out for myself what a real husband and father should be.

The anticipation of the birth of my son was exciting, and I enjoyed thinking about what he would look like and dreamed of holding him and rocking him to sleep. I wanted to be his hero, but I also feared I would disappoint him.

The thought of becoming a father would overwhelm me at times, and I would tell myself that our son would probably be better off if I were not in the picture. I was terrified of passing my issues, my bricks, along to him, an innocent babe.

As much as I was afraid of failure, though, I knew our child would need his dad. No one knew that better than I did. I had grown up without a father, a reality more painful than words can express.

I would not do that to our son.

Aging Out

As the time of our baby's birth grew near, Kristin did her best to dodge the minefield of my issues and prayed for me every night. She prayed I would understand that in the new life that was about to come into our lives I had a chance to be the dad I had never had.

Chapter 35

My Firstborn

I took great pride in trying to make the birth of our first child special. Along with going to all of the prenatal visits at the doctor's with Kristin, I saved all the bills, tried to laminate the ultrasound, and helped to paint and decorate the nursery in baby blue and yellow sailboats.

At some point, I decided I wanted to make a toy box and began to build it without a plan or a measurement. When I was finished, the toy box was twice as big as it should have been, so big I had to start over from scratch.

Kristin and I talked for a long time about what to name our son, and I was the one who suggested combining our two names. That's where "Kelton" came from. We already knew Kelton would also carry my grandpa's name, so Kelton Thomas it was.

A few weeks before her due date, Kristin and I went to her doctor's appointment and got some bad news. Her feet were swelling more than normal, she was having headaches, and her blood pressure was higher than it should be. Dr. Ebert told her she had a mild case of toxemia.

To avoid hurting the baby, he told her she would need to stay off her feet and get plenty of rest, and he wanted to see her in a week. We went home, and Kristin did just what the doctor had ordered.

The following week, her symptoms were worse. Dr. Ebert told us that the baby was still fine, but just to be safe—and to protect Kristin's health—he wanted to induce labor in a few days.

Kristin took the news calmly. I, of course, thought of all the bad things that could possibly happen to her or our baby and could hardly sleep, much less wait the few days for my son to be born.

My reaction is typical of someone who has had a childhood disturbed by tragedy and dysfunction and insecurity. Such children grow up to expect disaster around every corner because they have lived through the electricity being turned off on a cold night, through the cupboard going bare, through adults hitting them for no reason. Such children have been trained to expect crisis to be around every corner. It's like a strange form of post-traumatic stress.

And such a child still lived inside me.

On May 28, 1998, Kristin checked into Stillwater's hospital and was given a shot to induce labor. Every thirty minutes or so, a nurse came in to check how much Kristin had dilated. During one of the checks, the nurse told us she could tell that Kelton had lots of hair, but she could not tell us what color it was.

Kristin looked at me, and I said, with a smile, "Well, of course, it's black."

An hour or so later, Kristin gave birth to Kelton Thomas Carter. He weighed eight pounds, twelve ounces and measured twenty-and-a-half inches long. He also had the blondest hair I had ever seen—so much for my prediction.

Our beautiful biracial baby was absolutely perfect, and I couldn't have been more proud.

In the days and weeks to come after we took Kelton home, many a night found me unable to sleep, so consumed was I with fear, fear of ruining my son's life. More than once, Kristin found me standing over his crib just staring at him.

I loved my son more than I could ever have imagined, and although he was just a baby, Kelton Thomas Carter gave me both the strength I needed to get through those dark nights of uncertainty and the courage to try to overcome my lack of experience in the dad department.

When my son looked up at me, the world and all its troubles just disappeared.

My favorite thing to do was rock him to sleep, and in spite of the books that said not to, sometimes I'd hold him all night while he slept instead of putting him back in his crib. Being able to put Kelton to bed made me feel better about myself, proud that I was doing for my son what my dad never had done for me.

One night after putting Kelton to bed, I stood by the crib for a while just watching him sleep. Before I turned to go, I bent down and kissed him on the cheek. My whiskers must have tickled his face because his face scrunched up a little bit and he turned his head, but he didn't wake up. I walked out of the room thinking I just might be okay at this dad thing. In bed later that night, I found myself staring at the ceiling, thinking about how I would read to Kelton, teach him to throw a football, and ride a bike.

Before I could fall asleep, a cry broke the quiet, and without hesitation, I leaped out of bed and ran down the dark hallway and into my son's room. I picked him up and carried him back to our bedroom, stretched out on the bed, and positioned him on top of my chest. I rubbed his back and kissed the top of his head more times than I could count until both of us finally fell asleep.

That night seemed to last forever, but I remember it as the night I started to feel like a father.

Kelton was my firstborn, and while I might have reason to be insecure in the days and years to come, it was important for me to settle into fatherhood with some confidence so I could be a father that would make him proud. I loved Kelton, and no matter how badly I felt about myself, I would make sure that he always knew that I loved him. And that he could count on my always being there. I needed him just as much as he needed me.

The next morning, I watched the sun peek over the bedroom windowsill as a ray of sunlight came to rest on Kelton's face. Kelton wiggled a bit, blinked a few times, and then lifted his head. In doing so, he snuggled his mouth against my cheek for a few seconds before laying his head back on my chest and returning to sleep.

Another reservoir of fear and insecurities disappeared the moment my son kissed me on the cheek. I wasn't foolish enough to think I would never again have doubts about being a father or questions about my self-worth, but I knew that morning my son was pure love, and what he loved included me.

Kelton changed my life and gave me a sense of purpose. The way I handled things had yet to change much, but if I could accept Kelton's unconditional love, maybe, just maybe, someday I could accept Kristin's.

Chapter 36

A Seed Is Planted

Despite my good intentions for fatherhood, I spent way too much time in the summers away from home working at cheerleading camps. It wasn't an ideal job, but I got paid, and I enjoyed working with the kids. After a few camps, I started sharing my life story with the campers. After a few more, it became part of our routine to invite the cheerleaders and their coaches to hear how I had grown up.

The impetus behind this was that although we saw a lot of good in the young athletes we worked with at camp, sometimes they took what they had for granted.

On a few occasions, the entire camp showed up to hear me. I loved sharing and felt like I was making a difference with my story. I was one of the oldest camp employees, and although I could tumble with the best of them, I often felt I didn't belong.

For some reason, sharing my story with the campers and their coaches helped me feel a connection with them that I otherwise didn't feel. The one camp I will never forget was held on the campus of the University of Oklahoma in Norman. As I had done many times before, I shared my story the next-to-last night of camp with several groups gathered on the grass where we had practiced cheers all day. As I told the cheerleaders about the trials and obstacles I had faced as a kid, I also shared stories about people who had made a difference in my life and some of my regrets. I told them about how I had made fun of my little brother in front of his friends, only to lose him a few days later. I shared with them the story of the Christmas that my family forgot to buy me a present.

For some reason, the Christmas story left everybody in tears, especially a group of cheerleaders from Carl Albert Middle School, coached by Teresa Wilkerson. I had been impressed all session with not only how talented her kids were but also how incredibly respectful they were with each other.

After the speech, several of them came up to give me a hug and share how my story made them appreciate what they had. It made me feel like I was making a difference.

The last day of camp is typically a time of evaluations and awards, and we're usually finished by noon. This particular day, Teresa came up and told me her team wanted to meet with me right after camp was over. After the awards ceremony, I found the Carl Albert cheerleaders gathered in the parking lot.

"We have something for you," one of them said.

And with that, the captain of the squad handed me a blue sack with what looked like a small car sticking out the top.

"The girls came up with this idea all by themselves," Teresa said, with a grin.

I reached in and pulled out a white envelope. I opened the envelope and pulled out a card that read, "Merry Christmas, Alton."

Completely confused at this point, I looked at Teresa for an explanation.

"Look in the sack," she said.

I stuck my hand back in and pulled out the green tissue paper. I reached in again and pulled out a slinky, then a yo-yo, a Hot Wheels car, and a few other items meant for a little boy.

More puzzled than ever, I again looked to Teresa.

"Remember last night, when you told us about the time your family forgot to buy you a Christmas gift?"

"Yes, I remember," I said.

"Well, here are the gifts you should have gotten when you were a little boy."

Stunned, and without a second thought, I began to cry as the girls and Teresa stared at me, unsure if they were tears of happiness or if they'd embarrassed me or done something wrong.

They were tears of happiness.

I couldn't have been more grateful, and their simple act of kindness would eventually help me embrace the Christmas holiday again.

*****

Coming home from camp was the best because I missed my family more than my absences might have led them to believe. This time, I was no more home than I got a phone call from a woman who said she had heard me share my life story with the cheerleaders a few days earlier. The caller was a cheer coach who served as the student council sponsor for Elgin High School in Elgin, Oklahoma.

"Would you be interested in coming here next week and sharing your story?" she asked. She went on to explain that her student council was hosting a Make-a-Wish pep rally for a little boy named Drew. They intended to present him with a trip to Disney World.

"I'd be happy to come," I said.

The day of the rally, I arrived at a high school gym, which was already full of people. It was standing room only in the bleachers, and another few hundred people were seated in chairs on the gym floor. I was shown to the podium, and then the back doors of the gym flew open and in came Drew in a wheelchair being pushed by his mother. Behind Drew's mom was what looked to be his entire family.

The gym erupted in cheering and clapping. With each rotation of the wheels on Drew's chair, the cheers got louder. His mom rolled Drew right in front of me, parked his chair, and took a seat beside her son.

While the rest of his family seated themselves, it dawned on me that I had no idea why the student council was sending Drew to Disney World, so I quickly asked one of the students.

"Drew has brain cancer," the student council member said. "They don't think he has much longer to live. We're sending him and his family to Disney World because that was his wish."

I retreated to the podium with a lump in my throat and pain in my heart. The gym fell silent. Everyone was looking at me, waiting for me to speak. I had been told my job was to thank everyone for coming and then tell my life story, hoping it would inspire people to give a donation to pay the remaining balance on Drew's trip.

But I could not find a single word to say. I looked at Drew and my eyes filled with tears. I looked at his mom and wondered if she was mad at God for what was happening to her son. I wondered if they were scared, and I wondered how many days they had left together. All this I thought in a split second.

And as I stood there staring at Drew and his mom, I also thought what a mistake it was for me to be there. I had spent so many years being angry and feeling sorry for myself. And now I was supposed to talk to these people about growing up poor and in foster care? What did any of that matter to a dying boy?

Eventually, I decided to trust the woman who had asked me to speak. I looked out into the audience and I started telling stories of my childhood. I described in detail both the abuse and the wonderful people along the way who stepped up to love and help me. Several times, I had to choke back tears. I think the crowd thought I was crying because of my past, but in actuality, I was crying because every so often, my eyes would meet Drew's.

I finished the speech to a standing ovation.

As I walked away from the podium, one of the student council members handed me an envelope with my speaker's fee. As quickly as the student handed me the check, I handed it back.

"I cannot take this check, please give it to Drew's family," I said, and then I darted out the gym and ran to my car.

As I pulled away, I thought of all the times I had felt sorry for myself for what I didn't have, instead of being grateful for what I did have, instead of appreciating the little joys in life available to us all.

And I thought about Drew. And I thought about death. What would people say about me if they learned I was going to die soon?

If I gathered everyone I knew in a gym and picked five of them to speak, what would they say if they had to tell the truth about what kind of person I was? What would I say about me?

I almost slammed on the brakes at the thought.

I thought back on all the people I had mistreated, betrayed, or taken advantage of in one way or another. My list of regrets and poor choices was long.

By the time I pulled into Stillwater, I knew I needed to make some changes. It wouldn't be easy, and it wasn't likely anyone would instantly see a better me, but the seed was planted, and I was ready and willing to let it grow.

Chapter 37

Colin Arrives

May 8, 2000, saw us back at the Stillwater hospital with Kristin in labor again. We both knew what to expect this time, so we weren't surprised when a nurse came by to put a heart monitor on Kristin's stomach so she could track the baby's heartbeat.

The monitor was connected to a recording device with a speaker, so for the next few hours, our baby's heartbeat provided the background music as we waited for him to be born.

All was going well until about nine o'clock, when Kristin rolled over and the monitor fell silent.

The nurse came running, and she quickly began to look for the problem. Monitor plugged in? Check. Strap in the right place? Maybe. The nurse moved the monitor lower on Kristin's stomach. No heartbeat. She moved it again and again and again, trying several other positions. Nothing. Nothing. Nothing.

And then she rolled Kristin onto her back. Still nothing. Now frantic, the nurse called the front desk, asking for the head nurse to come quickly. In seconds, the head nurse was in the room, rolling Kristin back onto her side and moving the strap all over Kristin's stomach, again in search of a heartbeat. It had only been a few minutes, all in all, but I could feel the blood leaving my face, and my lips had started to tingle. My heart felt as if it were coming out of my chest. Another minute passed.

Woosh, woosh, woosh, woosh.

I have never heard a more welcome sound. Our baby's heart was beating again. The nurses apologized for the fright and assured us that the baby had never been in danger; they had simply had the monitor in the wrong place. It was good news, but we still found it difficult to relax after that. Thankfully, we only had a little longer to wait. At 10:31 p.m., Colin Dean Carter was born. He weighed eight pounds, four ounces and measured twenty-and-a-half inches long. He had tan skin and thick black hair, another beautiful baby boy.

I realized I was just as proud of him as I was when Kelton was born. And Colin was a big hit with his older brother. All Kelton wanted to do was to hold Colin, so we would set our oldest son on the couch and placed Baby Colin in his arms. Kelton would cuddle his little brother like that for hours, occasionally sneaking in a little kiss on Colin's soft forehead. Those precious moments will stay with me forever, and I am sure glad that I was around to witness them.

*****

Sometimes when I doubted my capabilities as a father, I would turn to writing, especially poetry. Writing poems for me was almost a way to dream about all that being a father could be. I know I've been a decent father to my boys, but I realized long ago I could have done so many things better.

Laying the boys down for bed at night when they were little remained special to me, and most nights after our bedtime ritual was over, I would get out pen and paper and write poems about what I loved about my Kelton and Colin. I would write about things I wanted to be a part of as they grew up. I had plenty of thoughts about their playing sports or making good grades in school. I also wrote about all sorts of things related to being a dad. Once the boys could talk, I jotted down things my kids said to me that made me happy. Eventually, I realized they were things I had never gotten to say to my dad, and they became music to my ears.

Music to My Ears

Hi Daddy
Come here Daddy
Sit next to me Daddy
Hello Daddy
Daddy did you hear me
Listen Daddy
Hold me Daddy
Why Daddy
Can you fix this Daddy
Can I ride with you Daddy
Where are you going Daddy
Daddy, what's that
Can I help you Daddy
Help me Daddy
Watch me Daddy
Daddy can I have a bite
Daddy is home
Can I have a hug Daddy
I'm Daddy's Boy
Thank you Daddy
Can I have a drink Daddy
Did you see that Daddy
I miss you Daddy
Read to me Daddy
I want to be like you Daddy
I love you Daddy
Daddy you are my Hero

As the boys grew older, it was obvious they were as opposite as two kids could be in most ways. Kelton loved eating meat, drinking milk, and watching Clifford the Big Red Dog and bull riding. Colin loved eating vegetables, drinking juice, and drumming on pots and pans with wooden spoons.

Colin was the one who loved to climb into our laps and kiss Kristin and me. Kelton loved to hug us but was rarely in one place long enough to do so. Older brother was also the talker, the one who repeated everything he heard and also said whatever was on his mind.

They both, however, loved being outdoors.

In public, our family drew its share of stares in the early years. It was like people were trying to figure out who belonged to whom. Once while grocery shopping, we had Colin in the front of a grocery cart and Kelton in the basket, and we no more than got inside Walmart when I noticed a woman staring at us. She continued to stare until we were within a few feet of her. As we passed her, she addressed Kristin: "Do your boys have the same dad?"

"Yes, they do, and this is their dad," Kristin said, and she pointed at me.

As we moved on, I had to resist the urge to go back and ask the woman if she knew how rude her question was. Kristin just shook off the comment and encouraged me to do the same thing.

Chapter 38

Mistakes Were Made

I was finding my way as a father and husband, but my days of making poor choices were by no means over, and sometimes my family suffered because of the terrible choices I made. I became unhappy with my job at the middle school (for reasons I no longer even remember), so I quit without telling Kristin beforehand or having a backup plan.

Coming home to face Kristin that day was not easy. We were struggling to make ends meet, coming up short almost every month. She couldn't believe I had once again quit a job without having one to replace it. "You should have discussed this with me before you quit, Alton," she said.

I knew she was right. Like so many other times in my life, I had neither thought that far ahead nor given any consideration to how my actions would impact anyone else, especially Kristin.

Ashamed of what I had done and feeling guilty, I spent the next few weeks feeling sorry for myself instead of throwing myself into the job search. Oh, I looked for a job, but only a few hours every day—I didn't make finding a job a full-time job, like I should have.

It became harder and harder to look Kristin in the face, knowing I had let her down and had put my family in jeopardy. The job search I had expected to take a few weeks turned into months, with no job in sight and bills piling up. When I finally could no longer deny how much trouble we were in financially, I managed to fight off my depression, and I started to spend all day, every day, looking for a job.

About that time, I ran into Leon Jones, an OSU police officer, who knew of an opening in his department. He suggested I apply.

"The hiring process takes some time," he said, "but I'll put in a good word for you."

I wasn't sure if I was cut out to be a police officer, but I was willing to do anything to get my family out of the situation I had put them in. A job was a job. So I went in and picked up an application, took it home, and filled it out.

The next morning I took the application back to the police department and was told they would be in contact with me if I made the first cut. I spent the rest of the day driving around town and obsessing about not having a job. By the time I headed home that evening, I had convinced myself I had no hope of being hired as a police officer.

I returned home to learn that we were completely broke and the electricity was about to be shut off. Some days, when it rains, it pours.

"Oh, and the air conditioner broke," Kristin added.

It was the middle of the summer; the temperature was averaging ninety degrees. The estimate for parts and labor to repair the air conditioner was $3,500. We didn't have ten cents. That night it was too hot to sleep in our rooms, so Kristin made pallets for all of us on the living room floor, and I set up two box fans, one on each side of the room. The fans didn't cool the hot air so much as they moved it around. That is how we slept the next few weeks.

Watching my wife and sons sleeping on the floor, sweating through the night, I felt like my childhood had come back to haunt me. Only this time, it was my fault. I had made the rash decision to quit my job, and now my family was suffering for it. My children were going through what I swore I would protect them from.

Aging Out

A few weeks later, Kristin's parents came to visit, and when they found out we didn't have air-conditioning, her father insisted on paying for the repairs. We, of course, refused to let him. "I'm not going to have Kelton and Colin sleeping in this heat without air-conditioning," he said. "At least let me buy a window AC unit."

And that's exactly what Dean did. He also installed it for us in the front room. I was truly grateful but also embarrassed that Kristin's father had had to do this for us. My pride, shaky at best, took a huge hit that day. Meanwhile, Kristin's mom asked if the boys could come home with them for a few days, and we agreed.

Kristin and I were left in the hot house, yet Kristin never complained nor said a word about the stifling heat. A few days later, I was telling a friend of mine about our air conditioner going out and how pricey the estimate to repair it had been. He asked me which heat-and-air company had looked at it. When I told him, he advised getting a second opinion. He said the same company had tried to overcharge him recently. I took his advice and called another local company. Troy Lambertus came right out, and it only took him a few minutes to assess the situation and tell me that an animal had chewed through a few wires and a switch needed replacing.

"It's an easy fix," he said, "and I can do it right now. It'll cost you about a hundred for parts and labor."

It was good news, but I had to tell him we didn't have the money to fix it right then.

Troy didn't even hesitate. "You have kids and a wife. You need an air conditioner in this heat," he said. "I'll fix it now, and we'll settle up later."

The repairman suddenly looked a lot like an angel in disguise. He made the repairs, and I thanked him several times before he left. A few days later, Cheryl and Dean brought Kelton and Colin home, and we borrowed the money from them to pay for the repairs.

The same day I paid Troy, I received a call from the OSU Police Department.

I had made it to the next round of interviews.

Sometimes when the sun shines, it shines everywhere.

Chapter 39

Officer Alton

The thought of my becoming a police officer was more than a little ironic. Most of my childhood, I had been taught to hate and avoid the police. My family history was a nightmare of handcuffs and sirens and arrest warrants. Seeing a relative hauled away to jail happened as often (and often with as much fanfare) as a rerun of *Cops*.

Since I was a little boy, I had always wanted to be the complete opposite of that kind of person, and now I stood on the cusp of literally doing just that. The job at Oklahoma State University promised a livable wage, health insurance, and respect in the community—all the things I needed for my little family.

The only thing that made me nervous was the thought of coming face to face with anyone from my family while on duty. I had dreamed of a better life than theirs, of being a better person than any of them had ever been, but I had still never turned my back on my family. In fact, much of the pain and turmoil in my life stemmed from a childlike desire to be accepted and loved by my mom, siblings, grandparents, uncles, aunts, and cousins. Given the powerful pull of family, is it any wonder that during my second interview with OSU, the interviewer made a point of asking: "If you saw one of your family members break the law, would you be able to arrest them?" My response was: "Yes, and without hesitation."

I realized my saying I could arrest my own brother or uncle so easily might have made it look like I hated my entire family, but I knew it was the right answer, the proper answer . . . the only answer.

Still, I couldn't help but wonder if the OSU police knew the extent of my family's troubles with the law and if that could keep me from getting the job I so desperately needed to feed my family and keep the lights on at home.

The next few weeks dragged by as I waited for the phone call that would mean I had been hired. When the call finally came, I was proud and excited to accept the job. I could not believe I had been chosen.

I was given a police uniform and a badge, Badge No. 41. I spent the next month in the classroom learning local and campus laws and ordinances and becoming familiar with the layout of the OSU campus, as well as how to fill out police reports, use a police radio, and what was expected of a police officer as far as conduct and professionalism standards.

The classroom part of my training complete, the next stop was the gun range, where I learned to use a firearm and shotgun. I had held a rifle several times before but had never fired a pistol, so I was more than a little nervous.

To carry a firearm, a police officer has to pass a shooting test at the firing range. To pass, 70 percent of one's shots have to hit the target. I fell short a couple of times, but with a little help from the firearms instructor, finally managed to pass with an 80 percent on the test. I was then assigned a field training officer named Dustin who I shadowed for another six to eight weeks in the field. After that, I was allowed to patrol campus by myself, while I waited to begin the police academy.

I loved patrolling campus, and I can't begin to tell you how good I felt about myself walking around in that uniform. I enjoyed the feeling of power that came with the uniform; it made me feel almost invincible. I did not, however, want to be one of those officers whose ego, insecurities, or love of power causes him to lord it over others or constantly remind people of the power of the badge. I still remembered the lesson my grandpa had taught me all those years ago: If you have to tell people you're the boss, you're not a leader.

I wanted to be an officer whom people respected and admired—an officer known for treating everyone with the respect a citizen or visitor to our town or this country deserves.

When the time came to go to the academy in Broken Arrow, Oklahoma, I learned I would be away from my family all workweek for eight-and-a-half weeks straight, coming home only on the weekends. This would be hard on me, hard on Kristin and the kids, and honestly, it would almost cause me to lose my way.

I didn't start off strong, either. The very first day of class, for some reason, the instructor called me forward and asked me to draw the outline of the state of Oklahoma on the chalkboard. Reluctantly, I made my way to the chalkboard at the front of the classroom. I grabbed a piece of chalk, and quickly did as he had requested. No questions asked.

I had no more than returned to my seat when the laughter from my peers started.

"Mr. Carter, it would appear that you've drawn the state backwards," the instructor said.

Sure enough, he was right. Oklahoma's famous panhandle was now next to Arkansas instead of New Mexico, if my drawing was to be believed.

The laughter got louder, and I was completely humiliated. My dyslexia had struck again.

Yes, it made for a difficult first day for me, but my mistake would soon be forgotten as others soon embarrassed themselves far worse in the weeks to come.

*****

The intense training and test taking—combined with missing my wife and kids—began to wear me down, and I began to consider quitting. I told myself I could go home and find another job. The old Alton of a few months ago probably would have done just that. Luckily, I still remembered the look on Kristin's face from the last time I had quit a job without another in hand. I had vowed I would never do that to her and the kids again.

And so I stuck it out.

At times, the training was grueling, not only physically but also mentally. I found the training videos of people killing officers disturbing and difficult to watch. The violence captured on the videos scared me so much I became paranoid and suspicious of everyone for a while.

But that wasn't the worst of it.

By far, the low point for me was the videos about child abuse cases. More than once, I had to get up and walk out in the middle of one of those. I had endured much of the same abuse as a child, and watching it on the screen made me feel as if I were reliving it all over again. Secretly, I sometimes worried what I might do if I were ever, in the line of duty, to come upon someone abusing a child.

Those feelings made me understand why police officers go through so much training to learn to be calm and controlled in dangerous and horrific situations—too often, they see the worst that mankind has to offer.

I finished the academy with the honor of being class leader, and I returned to Stillwater a certified police officer.

Chapter 40

Three Times a Charm

Given the headlines of the past few years, it will probably come as no surprise that not every officer with whom I worked behaved as a public servant should. Like every other profession, there were good and bad officers. Some officers were there for the right reasons; others were not. A few loved to hide behind the badge and intimidate people. Thankfully, most of the officers I worked alongside were honest men who took pride in keeping the faculty, staff, and students of OSU safe.

Unfortunately, those whom we swore to protect and serve weren't always appreciative. I loved patrolling the campus—meeting new people, seeing old friends, and being of service to students, faculty, staff, and visitors alike. And generally, at least during the day, those folks were extremely nice and polite to me.

However, as time went by, I found dealing with entitled and intoxicated students and adults to be much harder than I had ever imagined it could be. I can't begin to tell you how often I had to take being cussed out, threatened, and called names by the very people I had taken an oath to protect. I also found myself bothered by the high-handedness of some of my fellow officers. The poor pay and increasingly expensive health insurance for Kristin and the kids didn't help my job satisfaction either. After a year, I realized being a police officer was not what I had thought it would be.

*****

One day while on patrol alone in the OSU Student Union, I ran into an old friend and gymnastics mom, Martha McMillian, whose daughters I had previously taught tumbling. As head of the university's student academic center, she had helped many kids get into college, and on this particular day, as she had many times before, she suggested I go back to college and get my degree.

She knew what it took to do well in college, and I was flattered that she thought I had the right stuff. Unfortunately, as much as I wanted to return to school, I did not agree with her assessment of me. I didn't believe I was smart enough to pass the classes, much less earn a degree at OSU.

"I will come see you when I'm ready," I promised, but in reality, I had no intention of returning to school.

I also had no desire any longer to be a policeman. That realization coincided with Kristin's cousins, Lisa and Garth Williams, moving to Stillwater and offering me a job in their tire shop for the same money I was earning as a police officer—hard to believe given that one rarely has to put one's life in danger at a tire shop. I didn't have to think twice; I turned in my resignation to OSU.

Working for the Williamses during the day allowed me to make some extra money teaching gymnastics and tumbling classes at a local gym in the evening. I spent a year and a half working both jobs.

Kristin and I were catching up on bills, yet it was clear what I was making was not going to be enough to support the family in the long run. I needed to do more, and the only way to get a job that paid the salary we needed was to go back to college.

I thought about my conversation with Mrs. McMillian and decided to take off work and go see her, hoping she might know what my chances were of being accepted at OSU. I found her in her office, and we spent a few hours talking about my high school transcript and my past college experience. I explained I'd taken mostly remedial classes in high school and had graduated from Cushing High by the skin of my teeth, and then I confessed that I'd dropped out of college not once but twice. When she asked me why, I knew better than to give her a lame excuse.

"I just didn't finish," I said.

I wasn't sure what Mrs. McMillian was taking away from our chat, but the more we talked, the more I realized I couldn't go back to school. I couldn't do it. I didn't have it in me.

I must have said something to that effect because I remember Mrs. McMillian protesting. She said she knew I could do it, and if I would let her help me, she would do everything in her power to get me accepted and, maybe more important, through OSU with a degree. She persuaded me to let her see what it would take to get me enrolled. I left her office convinced that the next time we spoke, she would be telling me to forget any ideas I had of going to OSU.

But that's not what happened.

A week later, Mrs. McMillian called me and asked me to come see her. I had no more than arrived in her office when she handed me a class schedule. I was enrolled and starting school the next semester. In fact, Mrs. McMillian had put me in twelve credit hours, making me a full-time student.

I should have been happy, but I only remember feeling shock and fear in that moment. I was thirty-four years old and convinced I did not have the wherewithal to pass a college course.

"I'll do whatever I can to help you," Mrs. McMillian promised. "Come see me anytime."

She was so happy for me, I didn't have the heart to tell her she had unleashed a train that was destined to go off the tracks. Instead, I took my schedule, thanked her, and left with more fear in my heart than I had ever felt before.

I was getting a second chance. A lot of people in my position, even if someone like Mrs. McMillian made it possible, wouldn't have been able to afford to go back to school—not with a wife and two kids at home. Kristin and I spent the next few weeks crunching the numbers and applying for financial aid and student loans, and the math said it was possible, if I also kept teaching tumbling classes.

And so I became a college student again. Three times a charm, they say, and the first semester went better than I had thought it would, and I did far better than I had dreamed possible. I made the OSU dean's honor roll, which built my confidence for the next semester. The following semester, Martha enrolled me in fifteen hours, and the next, seventeen, and again, I made the dean's honor roll.

I wanted to finish as fast as I could so I could get back to work and supporting my family, so I enrolled in summer school and weekend courses to push me through quicker.

During my last three semesters, I worked at OSU in the athletic department. I supervised study hall and monitored athletes who needed extra supervision. In 2009, I proudly walked across the stage to accept my diploma, only to find out a few weeks later that a mistake had been made on my degree sheet. I was still a few hours short of graduating.

I had two choices: I could enroll in another semester or have my diploma say bachelor's of university studies instead of bachelor's in sociology. I decided I didn't care what was on my diploma; the important thing was having a degree, so I did not go back to college a fourth time. I had made family history again. After being the first in my family to graduate from high school, I was now the first to graduate from college, and soon I would start a job I was meant to do.

Knowing I had taken many a job just to pay the rent, it was my wife who suggested that it was time for me to do what I was put on this earth to do: work with young people in a setting where I could make a difference.

Luckily, there was at least one other person in Stillwater who agreed with my wife.

In 2008, I went to work at the First United Methodist Church as its director of youth ministries. I couldn't wait to use my education and talents to help the young people of Stillwater, but in the end, I was the one who was changed, in more ways than one.

I never saw it coming.

Chapter 41

Mom

My new boss, Mike Chaffin, and his wife, Leanne, soon earned a special place in my heart. The foster parents of two precious children, they are the foster parents I wish for every foster child. Watching the Chaffins with those kids never fails to warm my heart and in many ways helped me heal.

In the beginning, though, it was a struggle because I had never had nor known foster parents like the Chaffins. Leanne is soft-spoken and offers the kids the unconditional love that I longed for and never found in a foster home. She loves those two kids even when they try to push her away. Her patience, her willingness to wait until they are ready to let her in are something I wish every foster parent could see and learn from.

To this day, I also find something humbling about seeing Mike holding the kids' hands as they cross the street to church. The minute they grab his hands, he transforms into a gentle giant, one who exists to keep them safe.

There are no guarantees that the Chaffins or any other foster parent can ensure a child will grow up to be a stable and productive adult—much less a good father or mother, but the one thing I do know is that good foster parents offer foster children a chance.

*****

Come to find out, my new job was full of surprises, one being that I now saw my mom a lot more. She quickly—without asking for it or particularly wanting it—became my first project.

For years, I had been telling my mom that she needed to stop smoking. I didn't say it to be mean or controlling, I was just worried about her health. And rightly so, I thought. Yet whenever I broached the subject, she shot me down. "I like smoking, Alton," she would say. "I have no intention of stopping."

I would then remind her that smoking had claimed the lives of two of my uncles, her brothers. Such reminders of the cancer that had ravaged her brothers—she and Grandma had been the ones to care for my Uncle David and Uncle Thomas—always upset her, but never enough for her to stop smoking.

"You don't know what it's like," she'd say. "Quitting isn't easy."

She was right. I had no clue what being addicted to cigarettes was like, much less what it was like to try to quit smoking once hooked. Still, I tried to do my part to help her quit. I never gave her cash for fear she would use the money to buy cigarettes. Instead, if she needed food or her bills paid, I would always go buy the food or pay the bills myself.

Mom accused me of not trusting her, and she was right. I didn't, but I also didn't know what else to do. I wanted what was best for my mom, and I did not want to watch as cigarettes took her life.

Within a year, Mom's mental and physical health had deteriorated, the burden of constant family issues coupled with poor nutrition, and the smoking had turned into a toxic cocktail. She had been diagnosed with chronic obstructive pulmonary disease and was now unable to walk across the room without catching her breath. An oxygen tank and mask had become her constant companions.

On one particular Wednesday evening, I had decided to take the church youth group by to sing to my mom. Afterward, I went home to seven or eight missed calls from my older brother. Lavell often preferred to call several times in hopes of catching me instead of leaving a message, so I thought nothing of it. I was still scrolling through the call log when the phone rang.

The caller ID read, "Lavell." I picked up the phone to my brother's panicked voice: "Alton, you need to go over to Kesha's house. Shebba called. She found Kesha dead, upstairs!"

"Lavell, slow down. What did you say?"

"Shebba called and told me Kesha overdosed and is dead."

"Have you been over there to see if it's true?" I asked.

"No," he said.

I might have sounded oddly calm, but my family had a history of saying things like this. Kesha, in particular, was bad about getting mad at someone and then threatening to kill herself "so I can go be in heaven with my brother, the only person who ever cared about me anyway," as she put it.

Years of such Carter family drama had taught me to be wary of someone crying wolf. I was also upset because if what Lavell said was untrue, Kesha had sunk to involving her daughter Shebba into her playacting.

"I'll go by her house after I finish running a few errands," I told Lavell. "Meanwhile, why don't you go over there and see if you can figure out what's going on? If something is actually wrong, call me back."

That is why I was picking up bread at the grocery when Lavell called back and said it was true. Our sister was dead.

He had driven by my sister Kesha's house and seen police outside her door, and the police were not letting anyone inside.

"You need to get over here, Alton."

I arrived to find Shebba sitting on the hood of a car with a few other people and, as my brother had said, two police officers standing at my little sister's front door. One of the officers met me coming up the sidewalk and said, "Alton, I am sorry to tell you, but Kesha is deceased."

He put his hand on my shoulder and asked if there was anything he could do for me. It took me a second to fully grasp that my sister was dead. As I walked back to my truck, another car pulled up, and Kesha's son Shakeem jumped out and ran toward the house.

The same officer who had broken the news to me stopped Shakeem. At the officer's words, Shakeem started to cry and his body began to shake. His sister ran and embraced him while he screamed, "No! Not my momma!"

I stood and watched as the two of them wept. I wanted to go and take them in my arms, but I knew it would not be welcomed. We were not on the best of terms at the time.

As I got into my truck, I tried to imagine what life was going to be like without my sister. Kesha could be one of the sweetest people you would ever meet, but she was also moody and erratic. She almost always bought Kelton and Colin something for Christmas, but she was also likely to get mad a few days later and ask for it back. Still, she might have been the only person in my family to consistently think of my children.

Watching her from the sidelines, I had never fully understood why she struggled so. That she was full of life, there was no doubt, but she could also be the world's biggest drama queen. She had always battled depression and some sort of undiagnosed mental illness, which probably explained some of the highs and lows. At times, the depression could keep her in the house for days. Like my mom, she never quite got it right with a man, so far as I know. She had four kids by four different fellas, and many of the men were abusive. But Kesha loved her kids with all her heart.

Me, well, I loved my sister even though we couldn't seem to talk without ending up in an argument. She always ended such conversations by telling me that she hated my guts.

I never thought I would miss hearing that.

Looking back, I think we resented each other. I resented her because she treated her kids just like our mom had treated us: She put drugs and men before her kids, just like our mom had. And just like our mom, she didn't shield her kids from her poor choices. She resented me for getting out and making something of myself but also, I suspect, because she thought I now thought I was better than she was. If she'd only known.

I'm afraid I often came across as judgmental to my sister, when all I wanted was what was best for her and the kids.

I did what I could to help my sister, and it wasn't until she was gone that I gained a deeper understanding of how I probably came across to her and to her kids as they grew older. If my sister needed something and I helped her, it always came with instructions and advice.

I realize now that sometimes my sister just wanted my help, no questions asked.

I was good at being her big brother and trying to protect her, but I failed Kesha when it came to being her friend or giving unconditional help or love.

I was foolish in thinking that I could save my sister from herself by giving her things with conditions.

I left my sister's house and called Kristin to share what had happened. I figured someone had already told my mom, so I drove straight to the hospital. I found Mom crying, with the nurses doing their best to comfort her.

Mom insisted she needed to leave so she could take care of her daughter's body. It was heartbreaking to see my mom grieving from the loss of yet another child. They say the pain of losing a child is like no other. It's unnatural. Parents are not supposed to have to bury their children. My mom was about to do it for a second time.

Over the next few days, Mom helped plan the funeral from her bed in ICU. And all was fine until the doctors told her that she would not be able to attend the funeral. They feared if she left the hospital she, too, might die.

Chapter 42

Good-bye, Kesha

The day of Kesha's funeral, Mount Zion Baptist Church was filled with people who loved my sister, but the woman who gave birth to her was not there. Mom was still hospitalized, and medication would ensure that she went nowhere.

Pastor Miller gave Kesha a proper send-off, wrapping up his eulogy with a plea that we all love each other because life on this earth is short, sometimes shorter than we expect. His words brought people to tears, and that's when I realized I had yet to shed a single one for my sister.

I was numb, and I felt nothing save for maybe guilt. Did my inability to feel loss at such a dire moment mean something was wrong with me? Or was I just in shock—shocked that my little sister was dead and once again, just as when her twin had unexpectedly died all those years ago, I was cheated out of a chance to ever tell her I was sorry or that I loved her?

As the funeral service ended, I saw Coach Davis, the Stillwater High School basketball coach, and the entire Pioneer basketball team sitting up front. The boys were there to support JJ, Kesha's oldest son. Developmentally challenged, JJ had for years served, at Coach Davis's request, as the team manager for the Pioneer basketball team. The sight of those young men standing by their friend in his time of need was something to behold.

And I finally broke down.

*****

After the memorial at the cemetery, I took Kristin, Kelton, and Colin home, and then I headed to the hospital to check on Mom. I knew that when she woke, she would be devastated to have missed Kesha's final good-bye. I wanted to be there to comfort her.

In the end, she was relieved to hear the funeral had gone well, but I could tell she was worrying over something.

"Mom, what's bothering you?"

She told me she had given some relatives the keys to her apartment so they would have a place to stay while they were in town for the funeral. Now she was having second thoughts about it. She wanted me to go get the key back for fear someone might steal her things.

I stayed with her a little longer and then drove over to her house. I arrived to what looked like a huge block party.

People were coming in and out of her house. More people were standing in her front yard drinking and smoking weed. All the street parking spots in front were taken, so I drove around the block until I found one. By the time I walked to the house, a fight had broken out between two of the people at the party.

Now about twenty people were engaged in fights all over the yard. Others were cussing and screaming at the top of their lungs. Within a few seconds, it turned into an all-out brawl. I yelled at everyone to stop, but no one seemed to hear me. I started to physically pry people apart, but as soon as I separated one fight, another would start. This continued for several more minutes as I pleaded with people to stop fighting.

Police sirens in the distance finally got their attention. Everyone took off in different directions, jumped in their cars, and drove away. When the police arrived on the scene and started to question the neighbors, I ducked into my mom's house and found her keys lying on the coffee table.

I grabbed the keys, locking the doors and windows on my way out. When I returned the keys to Mom at the hospital that night, I did not tell her what I'd found there—or how scared and helpless it had made me feel.

She had been through so much already.

I loved my mom and my family, but in a way that was not particularly healthy. I wanted to save them from themselves, and it was silly to think that I could. One of the ways I was able to ease some of my frustration about my family was to write poems. Here is how I felt the evening I broke up the fight in front of my mom's.

To the Core

Every beat of my heart tells a descriptive story of what I love

Every breath that I take cries out of hope and a gasp for life

Every scar on my body is a blueprint of the pain I have endured

Every tear in my eye is weighted with betrayal

Every smile on my face hides the scared little boy that is hidden inside

Every drop of sweat that falls from my brow reflects guilt from my past

Every wrinkle on my forehead shows a timeline of what I have been through

Every callus on my hand reveals the labor I have put in to survive

Every ounce of my muscle, built by the heavy load I have carried

Every thought in my head is influenced by the circumstances that surround me

Every pint of my blood contains strength that will see me through

Every fingernail on my hand carries dirt from what I am ashamed of

Every thought in my mind is influenced by what I missed out on

Every day is a new day and I have come too far to give up now

I would give anything to not have thoughts like this, but I understand where they come from. I write to have some sort of release from the pressure of them. I know that not to deal with my feelings risks their consuming me and puts me at risk of self-destructing.

The next few days, mom struggled to hold herself together. At any given moment, she would burst into tears; nothing I could say made a dent in her sorrow. Most of the time, she would cry without saying a word, but occasionally she would talk about Kesha and Watell or tell stories about the two of them as children.

She became worried about Kesha's apartment and wanted me to go by to make sure no strangers were living there. I drove over there and found the landlord outside Kesha's place, talking to the neighbors. He needed her stuff out fast, and I promised we'd have it gone within a couple of days.

I called my brothers, Dejohn and Lavell, to help me with the apartment; both begged off. I called Shakeem and Kentell next; both of them begged off as well, saying that given what had happened to their mom, they could not go back there. I understood and told them I'd take care of it.

"Is there anything of your mom's that you'd like me to set aside for either of you?" I asked.

Both gave me the same answer as my brothers: We don't want anything.

Chapter 43

Outcast

I found Kesha's apartment all but destroyed. Holes peppered the walls, trash covered the floors, all the windows were broken, and the back door had been kicked in. Upstairs, my sister's bedroom floor was covered in six inches of trash and piles of dirty clothes. Both dressers were turned over and missing their drawers. The clean clothes in her closet had been stripped from the hangers and now hid the closet floor.

In her other bedroom, I found hundreds of dollars of what I presumed to be stolen property: televisions, CDs, and radios, with PlayStations and game consoles piled in the closet. The place looked as if it had been vandalized. My sister's apartment was never spotless, but it had never looked like this before. I spent a few hours picking up trash and hauling it to the apartment complex's dumpster.

With the trash gone, I went home to shower so I could go back to the hospital to visit Mom. The next morning, I told Kristin about my crazy day at my sister's and that I wanted the boys to come help me clean. She promised to bring them by after school to help. I headed back to the apartment to start on the piles of dirty clothes, only to begin to notice all sorts of pill bottles scattered all over the house—most of them at least half full. Not sure what they were, I put them one by one into a Rubbermaid container instead of tossing them. By the time I had collected all the prescription bottles, the ten-gallon Rubbermaid container was full to the brim.

Kristin brought the boys by to help me as promised, but when one of them asked if this was where Aunt Kesha had died, I realized they were no more comfortable in her house than her own kids had been. And so I let them go home. I continued until sunset, when I finally called it quits for the day. I didn't mind being alone in Kesha's house during the day, but I had no desire to be there at night.

When I went to visit Mom at the hospital that night, I found her on the phone with my brother Lavell, and it was obvious he was telling her something she didn't want to hear. She hung up and looked at me with sadness in her eyes.

"Lavell says there was a fight at my house after the funeral." It was a statement not a question. She started to cry. "Why would my family do that?"

I knew that question wasn't aimed at me but at a higher power.

Sadly, neither God nor I had an answer for her that night.

"I don't know, Mom, but you need to stay calm and focus on getting better. It's over and done."

She looked square at me: "Did you know about the fight?"

"Yes, I did, and I wasn't going to tell you because I didn't want to upset you. I don't know why Lavell would tell you, knowing there was nothing we could do about it now and that it would only upset you."

Mom looked up at me again and said, "Because he is my son and he is looking out for me."

I should have kept my mouth shut. But I was so frustrated with Lavell and hurt by what my mother's words implied I didn't do. Instead, I piled more pain on a woman who had just lost her little girl.

"Since Lavell called you and told you about the fight, did he tell you he was there and fighting just like everyone else? Lavell is one of the main reasons the fight started because he was drunk and screaming at people."

As soon as I said that, I realized what a terrible mistake I had made. Her reaction was a flashback to my youth, to the times when my uncle had hurt me or Grandma had cursed at me and I had had the gall to complain. She got mad.

Not at Lavell, but at me.

"You never liked your brothers and sister; you're always so quick to judge, always acting like you're better than the rest of us."

The words just spewed out of her.

I stood frozen until she screamed: "Get out of my room—I can't stand you!"

It was not the first time I had heard such accusations from my mother or others in my family. Indeed, I had long since grown immune to them. Yet, for some reason, on this night, seeing my mom hooked up to machines, tiny and helpless, each word hurt.

I walked out of the room and came face to face with a nurse in the hall. My hurt must have shown on my face because the nurse stopped me and said, "Your mother is sick and under a lot of stress with your sister's passing. Don't take it personally; she doesn't mean what she says."

She might as well have been talking to a pillar of salt.

"If she's going to talk to me like that, I'm not coming to see her."

I walked out of that hospital vowing never to visit my mom in the hospital again. It had been a long day, and I was exhausted and emotionally drained. I felt as if the rest of the family had deserted me, leaving me to take care of everything when it came to our sister and Mom all on my own.

I'm sure a therapist could have a field day with the irony of the good son being also the disavowed son, but the reality was actually much darker.

I was also doing my very best to suppress old memories that could slay me if I allowed them to surface. I went home, sank into the couch, and tried my best to go to sleep. I tossed and turned all night. I had never felt so alone, although in actuality, I was alone with my demons only because I chose to be. I told myself I wanted to protect Kristin and the boys from my family, so I did my best to shield them from the never-ending dysfunction. But while I shielded them from the chaos on that side of the family, they saw the pain from the dysfunction that infested me. I did my best to hide my pain from Kristin, Kelton, Colin, and our church family. Not wanting people to think I was weak, I tried like heck to conceal what was going on inside me.

Within a matter of days, I was also back visiting my mom in the hospital.

I would never forget what she had said that awful night, but I would err in love, as Pastor Miller had advised.

Chapter 44

The Verdict

The damage Mom had done to her lungs from smoking cigarettes all those years was severe and, at this point in her life, irre-
versible, from what the doctor had said, but I will always think that
losing Kesha is what started the downward spiral.

And there was no denying, the doctor's verdict was dire: My
mother's condition would grow worse and worse until the point that
she would eventually suffocate to death.

It was not a death one would wish on an enemy.

The diagnosis made me both furious and tearful. Furious because I'd tried for years to get Mom to quit smoking. Tearful because
I knew without a doubt that my mom would soon die a terrible
death. And I would have to watch.

I couldn't even imagine what it was like for my mom to get such
a death sentence, to know that the window to making her dreams
come true was closing.

Hers had been such a hard life. Five children. No husband.
Most, if not all, of her life relying on a government check to help
her make ends meet. The seven hundred or so dollars in assistance

or food stamps had never lasted long: a little for groceries, a little for rent and bills, a little for the loans mom had taken out to pay off my brothers' court costs. By the middle of the month, Mom was usually out of money and struggling to make it to the end of the month.

I thought about all the guilt and regrets Mom had to be holding onto. Mom was a religious person who prayed, read the Bible, and often quoted Scripture. I couldn't help but wonder if she blamed God for all the bad things that happened to her, but talking religion with Mom was a double-edged sword, and nothing good ever came from the two of us trying to figure out whose side God was on.

Trying to sway her once with the God card, I tried telling her that God would not approve of the way my brothers took advantage of her, making her pay the cost of their mistakes when she didn't have enough funds to keep her own lights on.

Her response: "The only reason you have what you have today is because God blessed you more than the rest of our family. They'd do better if you'd just pray for them."

Sadly, I think my mom convinced herself that I was chosen by God to succeed and the others were left without any blessing at all.

The doctor's news brought to the surface old memories and unresolved issues with my mother long buried deep within me. I suddenly resented her more than I ever had before, while at the same time I went into hyperdrive trying to win her approval before she died, mostly by doing whatever I could to take care of her.

For the next six months, I would do anything for my mom except hug or kiss her. My inability to display physical affection to her had nothing to do with her illness or shortcomings as a mother and everything to do with what she had done to me physically as a little boy. I was remembering, and I couldn't outrun the memories, and so when I got home, I wrote the following as part of a longer rumination on the mother-son bond:

A Mother's Gift to Her Son

Besides love, the greatest gift a mother can give her child is memories. My life was full of memories, but I didn't know how different they were from other kids' until I became much older.

Aging Out

My mom gave birth to me, loved me, and took care of me while I was a baby. I can't remember, but I assume that when I was young she did for me all the things a mother was supposed to do.

I know that I longed for her attention as I grew older, but I don't remember getting it. I would play in front of her so she could see me use my imagination. I would share with her my art from school, hoping that she would be impressed. I know now that it wasn't normal for a mom to watch her child play through the empty pill bottle. I know now that there was something wrong when my mom looked past my artwork so she could see what outfit she was going to wear that night.

When I had a bad dream, I ran to her, but she wasn't in her room. When I wanted something to eat and I ran to the kitchen, I was always disappointed, as I found nothing to stop the pain in my stomach. If I fell and scraped my knee, she was never there to kiss it and make it better. Instead, she was in the bedroom, waiting on some stranger hand and foot.

When I needed discipline and correcting for something I had done wrong, I got beatings with belts, hangers, extension cords, and sticks. A mother's gift to her son should be something that makes him appreciate life. My memories of childhood should be filled with stories of Mom coming to the rescue and Mom hugging me when I did something cool. I should have memories of my mom rocking me to sleep, kissing me good night, and wishing me sweet dreams.

Instead, my mother's actions replaced my sweet dreams with nightmares that haunt me to this day. I was afraid of my mom because her touching me was not the way a Mom should ever touch her son. Her affection made me hate every inch of my body. Her house was not a safe place because there was no room that could protect me from the gift she gave me. My mother's gift was saturated with betrayal, lies, neglect, and emptiness. And that is the gift my mother gave to her son.

I spent those last months with my mom thinking about and replaying in my head all she had done to me in the past—all while taking care of her. It was not an easy juggling routine.

My hope, however, was that in the act of caring for her, I would gain some sort of acknowledgment, recognition, or apology for the line she had crossed, something that would bring me a little peace.

I wasn't sure I could forgive or forget what she had done to me— even if she could ever bring herself to acknowledge it in the light of day—but I thought maybe if we could create some good new memories, it would help to ease my pain.

Knowing that the end for her was near, I didn't feel like I had any other option.

Chapter 45

Falling Down

The lingering issues with my mom ensured that my remaining time with her would be complicated. Unfortunately, my unease also followed me home.

I was hurting, yet unwilling to let my mom see that when I was with her. Instead, I showed it to Kristin and the boys.

Kristin did her best to listen and comfort me, but no matter what she said, it was always the wrong thing. I would demand that she listen, and she would listen, but then I would get mad that she didn't talk. When she did talk or give me advice, it was never what I wanted to hear. I told myself she didn't understand what I was going through, but then again, how could she?

It was a no-win situation for her, so she did the only thing she could do, and that was shut down emotionally to protect herself from me.

As for the boys, well, it wasn't like I could tell my boys what had happened to me as a kid. Well, at least not all of it. I worried about what they would think of me if they knew, so I kept it between Kristin and me.

I know now that one of the many mistakes that I made was not telling my kids what happened to me. They would have understood, and they would have loved me no matter what. They loved me when I locked myself in my room and cried for hours. They loved me when I screamed and yelled at them or Kristin for the silliest things. They loved me when I slammed the door on my way out of the house at night. They loved me when I talked to other people about my personal problems, when I should have been sharing my secrets with them.

Like so many others who have been where I've been, I didn't want to hurt anymore, but I also was not willing to do what it took to heal. Instead of seeking help from a professional, I just dug myself a deeper, darker hole by hurting the people who loved me more than anything.

To make matters worse, every day I spent with my mom seemed to uncover something else I had forgotten.

Foolishly, I tried to keep myself occupied round-the-clock so I wouldn't have to think about my problems. It was exhausting, and I soon tired of pretending to have it all together. I also wasted a lot of energy trying to prove to the church that my faith was strong—and that I could handle everything going on in my life with my mom and the death of my sister by myself.

I remember after another restless night calling the church to say I wouldn't be in the office for a few days because I was taking care of my sister's stuff. Three people from church, our Senior Pastor Mike Chaffin, Ed Davis, and Janelda Lane, offered to help, but I refused. Mike said he could get some men to help, while Janelda and Ed suggested that the church youths and their parents would show up en masse to help me.

I told them no for two reasons: I was embarrassed about how filthy and full of bugs the house was and did not want anybody from the church to see my sister's house and talk about it behind my back, and I was mourning and trying to come to grips with the loss of a sister with whom I had not been on the best of terms. Our last three phone calls had ended with her cussing me out and my hanging up on her; our final call included her telling me she hated my guts and was going to kill herself. I could only hope that in taking care of the loose ends Kesha had left behind by myself, I would find some sort of closure.

What were the odds that my last conversation with both my brother and sister would be negative? It was something I was going to have to live with the rest of my life.

Maybe I couldn't have controlled what they did or said, but I could have responded differently. It was my fault and my fault alone for hanging up on Kesha, and it was my fault and my fault alone that I had made fun of Watell in front of his friends the last time I saw him.

I chose to do what I did. I knew even as I was doing it that it wasn't the best choice, but it is how I chose to handle each of those situations. The only difference was that I was just a boy when I hurt Watell; I was a grown man when I hung up on Kesha.

Life doesn't always give you a second chance.

I'm proof of that.

Cleaning my sister's house didn't take away my guilt or pain. It was too late for me to be a good big brother to Kesha, but maybe I could be a better son to my mom.

*****

Mom's health had worsened, just as the doctor had predicted, and so she was moved to a hospital in Oklahoma City. The more time I spent with her there, the more I realized how much of the past I was holding onto.

I needed to forgive her for both of our sakes, but I wasn't sure if I had it in me to do such a thing. I had let my feelings about the past fester for so long, I didn't know how to let them go—in a strange way, they were the scaffolding on which my current life hung.

There was no way Mom could undo what she had done to me, and I was under no delusion that I could forget it either. I just realized I needed to forgive her anyway or I would spend the rest of my life in a cell of my own making. Convinced that if I were to tell her specifically why I needed to forgive her she would deny it, I decided

I would just tell her that I forgave her. The very next visit, I walked straight into her room and up to her bed and said, "Mom, I forgive you."

She did not respond, but I knew she had heard me.

I said it again. "Mom, I forgive you."

She looked at me for a few seconds without making eye contact, then looked away and fixed her eyes on the wall.

I was not expecting her to tell me she was sorry or even to acknowledge that she had wronged me. Nor was I surprised that she couldn't look me in the eye. I just needed to tell her face to face that I forgave her so I could move on and begin to heal.

I wish I could tell you that telling her gave me instant peace.

But it didn't.

In fact, it actually seemed to reopen the wound I was trying so very hard to close. Saying "I forgive you" to my mom was one of the hardest things I have ever done. I didn't know what to expect afterward. I had hoped for healing; instead, I came to realize I had to deal with my past if I wanted to heal. Forgiving my mom, well, that was just step one.

To this day, I am still taking it one step at a time.

In the end, it forced me to deal with a major issue in my life. Now Mom knew I remembered what she had done to me, and yet I was there to take care of her. They call it unconditional love.

Chapter 46

The Prodigal Son

Saying good-bye to my mom was never going to be easy, but in the end, the bricks she still carried made it worse than it had to be.

Fear played its role as well, I suspect.

And I still hadn't quite learned the lesson the universe had been trying to teach me.

The visit had not been going terribly well, even with one of her grandsons and his buddy there with me, and so after about twenty minutes of curt one-word answers from my mother, I told her we'd be going so she could get some rest.

As we headed out the door, I looked back at her one last time and caught the most hateful look in her eye. The muscles in her face were pulled taut and her lips were twisted.

"I know what you're doing to me, Alton," she said.

"Mom, what are you talking about?" I asked.

She lifted her left arm up and pointed a finger at the window. "I know you're trying to put me back in the home outside the window."

"Mom, we're on the second floor, and there's no home outside the window."

She stared out the window and said, "You are a liar, and I know you're trying to kill me. You've been trying to kill me this whole time."

I stopped in my tracks, confused by why she was saying such awful things to me.

"Mom, we are leaving, and you have no right to talk to me that way."

She took her eyes off the window, looked at me again, and replied, "Then get out of my room and don't ever come back. I hate you anyway."

I'm sure I flinched, but I was trying to hold it together for Colin and Steven.

I headed down the hall toward the elevator, with Steven and Colin on my heels, trying to see how I would react. I kept my head down looking at the floor.

When we arrived at the elevator, Steven said, "She had no right to be mean to you, Alton. You are the only one in your family who is taking care of her."

It took every ounce of strength to keep from crying in front of the boys. I took Steven to his house and then drove home, where I went straight to my bedroom and cried for what seemed like hours, all the while trying to figure out why my mother would say such a thing to me. I don't know what happened to my siblings after I left home at age nine. Truth be told, I don't know all that happened to them or to my mother in the years that followed while I was at the boys ranch and then various foster homes and college.

I only know that within a few years, my youngest brother was dead, none of my other siblings made it past ninth grade, and my mother seemed on a long, slow downward spiral.

I don't claim to know all the awful details.

I only know there had to be a reason why my mother always said the same thing whenever I took to criticizing my siblings and their choices: "Because your childhood was better than theirs, you cannot understand what they are going through."

That statement should have given me pause. My childhood after leaving home was no picnic, but if my mother was to be believed, those I had left behind had experienced much worse. I believe now she was asking me not to harden my heart against them.

If I had not been so distraught, maybe I would also have remembered how my grandpa began to see and fear things when he was near the end. We can't hold what sick or elderly people say as they are fading away because rarely is it the person we love actually speaking . . . it is the meds or the disease or the fear. Our job is to see past all that to the person inside, the person we love, the person who needs our love and compassion as he walks on.

At about ten o'clock that night, I got a call from the ICU. It was a nurse telling me to come to the hospital as soon as possible because mom had taken a turn for the worse.

Twenty minutes later, I walked into Mom's room; she was unconscious in the bed with a plastic mask over her mouth and nose. She was breathing shallow breaths and would not respond to me.

"What's wrong?" I asked the nurse.

The nurse explained that the infection was now attacking my mom's organs.

"It's time to call the family and have them come say their good-byes," the nurse said.

"Is there any chance she'll regain consciousness?" I asked.

The nurse shook her head, saying Mom was unlikely to wake up again.

"How long does she have to live?"

The nurse replied, "I would be surprised if she made it until the morning."

A machine was helping my mother breathe at this point, and I watched her and it for several minutes, scared that I would see her take her last breath.

Helpless like I had never been before, I wanted to be there for my mom as she left this world, but I could not watch my mom die.

Eventually, I started to make the calls to let the family know Mom was dying and it was time to come say good-bye. I called and called, but no one answered the phone. By 8:00 a.m. the next day, I had left dozens of messages on my relatives' phones, begging them to come to the hospital. No one of them ever called me back.

At 9:00 a.m., two of my mother's friends arrived at the hospital. I left her in their care, explaining that I did not want to be there to watch her die. Mom's face was losing its color, and she was now breathing only once or twice a minute. It would not be long now.

I left the hospital, got in my car, and headed for Strode's Funeral Home; I had only made it three blocks when I got a call from one of the ladies with Mom.

"Alton, Glendola is gone."

I turned around and went back as quickly as I could. The nurses were working on Mom when I arrived, and so I waited with her friends outside her room until they were done.

That first look at my mom when the nurses let us back in was the first time in my entire life that I had seen my mother at peace. No more breathing machines, heart monitors, or IVs stuck in her arms, Mom looked as if she had fallen asleep and might wake at any moment.

Her friends were touching her face and fixing her hair, but all I could do was look. When they were done, I reached down, took her hand, and removed the ring that my grandma had given her. I removed the one thing that could have started a family feud before my mother's body could even leave the hospital.

I wanted to hold onto this feeling of peace as long as I could.

*****

When it came time to plan the service, Mike not only agreed to do the service, but Ed helped me with the program. I had shared some of my issues with Ed, but I wasn't sure how much Mike knew about my relationship with my mom.

When Mike asked me about my mom so he could work on the eulogy, I told him I didn't want him to talk about Mom like she was a saint, but it'd be nice if he could acknowledge that there had been some good times. Mike said he understood and ensured me he could deliver an appropriate message.

My church family started a funeral fund, and within a few days, they had collected enough money to pay for the entire funeral.

When I found out about the fund, I talked to Ed about it. I told him I didn't want the church to pay for the funeral because I wanted to do it myself.

I didn't tell Ed at the time, but I was embarrassed at the very thought that anyone might have to help us at one of the watershed moments of a family's life. And if I'm being completely honest, to some degree I also wanted to make a point to my family. I wanted to show them that in spite of how they had treated me through the years, I had not forsaken them—I was still taking care of them. This prodigal son still ached for his joyous homecoming.

Ed would have none of it.

"The church paying for the funeral is not about you, Alton. It's about the congregation wanting to do their part because we love you."

It was more than I deserved, and I am not sure the church members to this day know how much I appreciated it. Kristin and I were practically broke, our family budget having been stretched thin trying to cover both our and Mom's bills.

Chapter 47

Remove the Thorn

My mother's funeral service went off without incident—strange praise, but only if you don't know my family. The funeral dinner in the church hall was marred only by an uncle who showed up drunk.

All in all, pretty good.

Wanting the family to have a chance to be together, just us, I invited everyone to my house for an 8:00 p.m. gathering with the promise of food. I also told them I would not tolerate any drugs or alcohol in my house.

Almost forty-five minutes late, my relatives started to show up, most of them high on pain pills. My family does not deal well with pain. We are good at causing pain and hurting each other, but we are not good at feeling pain. I knew pills or alcohol was how most of my relatives would usually deal with bad news or a bad day. I just couldn't believe they would show up to my house in that condition on the day of my mother's funeral, especially after I had asked them not to.

About fifteen after nine, Janelda and her son, Gabe, stopped by to drop off a few things I had left at the church. Normally, I would have been too embarrassed to have nonfamily see my family in action, but it was almost as if I needed a witness. I wanted someone outside of my family to see the way my family handled life's defining moments.

Janelda and Gabe joined Kristin, Kelton, and Colin on the floor, and together we watched a pageant of people dropping food and spilling drinks while others struggled to be understood despite their slurred speech or not to pass out while walking across the room.

It was obvious that Janelda and Gabe had never seen such a display by adults before, and I regretted having exposed my own children to such a scene. I felt especially sorry that my four grade-school-aged cousins had to see their parents in that condition, but was more horrified when the oldest of the four matter-of-factly told me that the adults were all on Xanax and her own mom had taken six Xanax pills before coming to the wake.

The little girl then told me that this was life for her every single day. All I could do was hug her and tell her I was sorry; inside, I damned the cycle of substance abuse that held my family in its grips.

My family didn't stay much longer. Right after Janelda and Gabe left, my relatives cleared out, too. I told one and all that if I saw anybody who was high try to drive, I would call the police and have them arrested. Kristin and I asked if the kids could stay with us, but the adults insisted that the kids leave with them. I followed them outside and made sure each car had a sober driver behind the wheel.

I went to bed thinking about my younger cousins and how they were being raised just like we had been.

*****

Now that Mom was gone, I thought I would be able to move on. I thought the pain from my childhood would begin to fade. I thought my nightmares would end. I expected to feel some relief. But the days after Mom's funeral actually brought more frustration and confusion than I had ever had before.

And then I realized what was wrong: I had been mad at my mother my entire life, and now that she was gone, I had no one to be mad at any longer, but I was left with what remained: my brothers, my cousins, my aunts and uncles. And our last family gathering on the night of the day we buried my mom had made one thing quite clear to me: Believing you can change someone who doesn't want to change will push you to the edge of insanity.

I have spent my whole life wanting to help my family—giving advice, leading by example, showing up when I am needed, even when the person who needed me has let me down so many times before. Still, no matter how hard I tried, things remained the same.

I know my family, like my mother always did, believes I think I am better than they are. The truth is, my outsider perspective just allows me to see the cycle they are trapped in. The cycle of domestic violence that has been passed down from generation to generation. The cycle of thinking that all whites are out to get us and keep us down. The cycle of neglecting and abandoning children who not only crave but need stability. The cycle of crime and prison that has infested the very soul of too many in our family.

I was witness to it all. I grew up watching my relatives pass down the "victim" card. I watched my grandparents enable my aunts and uncles to the point of disability. I watched my aunts and uncles pass this on to their children, who are now passing it on to their children. At times, I have tried to separate myself from my relatives with the hope that things would change. I told myself that keeping them out of sight, out of mind would free me from obligation and responsibility. When that didn't work, I tried to change those who seemed to need to change the most.

I tried to change them with love and encouragement. I tried to change them with hate and judgment. But despite my best efforts, I failed. I failed so much trying to change them that it seemed as if failure became a member of my family. Only now do I see that the reason why change never came was because they didn't want to change.

They don't want to change because they believe that life is supposed to be the way it is for them. They believe that crime, abuse, and excuses are a part of every household. Sometimes I think they believe that everyone lives in a family as dysfunctional as ours. Other times, I think they want to reap the benefits of change without having to put forth the effort to make the changes that bring happiness and contentment.

It took many years for me to realize that I cannot change my family because they do not have the tools to change at this time—and they may never find them.

With that realization, I knew I had to arrive at a place where I could truly forgive my mom and my sister or my life would be a living hell until the day I died.

Yes, Mom and Kesha had made terrible choices when it came to raising their children, but thus far, it was me who had spent his entire life bitter. Neither was anything of which to be proud.

My bitterness had so far brought me nothing but grief. I decided going forward that I would do my best to focus on the good things about them both and all the times they had made me laugh.

*****

In the wake of my mother's death, there were also fences to mend at home. I had been gone a lot while taking care of Mom, and unbeknownst to me, I had put my marriage at risk.

It took a huge argument with Kristin for me to realize what damage I had done—not only during the recent spell with my mom but through the years.

Kristin rarely talks about her feelings, and when she does, she only needs a few words. I, on the other hand, talk and write about my feelings all the time and at great length. What I had failed to do, however, was share where my pain came from. I often talked about my feelings getting hurt but rarely explained what caused it.

This particular argument was different because for the first time, Kristin told me how I had made her feel from time to time. She believed for the most part that we had a good marriage, but then she confessed that when I slipped into certain moods, it was very difficult to take.

She also reminded me that while Kelton and Colin truly loved me, they needed a better Alton. They deserved a better Alton.

Aging Out

"You are a great man and a lot of people love you," she said, "but your past is killing you, and it's starting to affect our marriage and your relationship with your children."

People like to say that you need to hit rock bottom before you can begin to recover, I would have sworn I'd hit rock bottom in that hospital room listening as my mother told me she hated me, the last words she would ever say to me.

But I was wrong.

Kristin had held up a mirror, and I did not like what I saw.

But I knew my wife was right.

Too often, I was angry because anger comes easy to me. I had been angry for most of my life. Now I suspected the anger covered a deep fear.

I was scared of what would happen if I dug too deeply into my past. But my wife was telling me that just like one would do with a festering thorn, I had to dig out whatever it was I feared before it killed me and destroyed our marriage.

Chapter 48

Seeking Help

I feared so many things, I didn't know where to begin.

Writing my first book, *The Boy Who Carried Bricks*, fulfilled a lifelong dream of mine, and it had proven therapeutic as well. When an early reader copy was well received by my church family at First United Methodist in Stillwater, I was a man on top of the world.

But digging up my past so I could put it on the page had also triggered emotions I wasn't prepared to handle. My editor had warned me this might happen, and now it was—just as she'd predicted.

Twenty-four hours after one of the best days of my life—outside of meeting Kristin, our wedding, and the births of our sons, I was once again on unstable ground.

The morning after that big book signing party with my church family, I had an appointment to have my teeth cleaned, and it was probably telling that the first thing Dr. Spaulding said when he saw me was: "Is everything okay?"

I assured him everything was fine but sensed that he didn't believe me. Still, he let it go. I followed him back to an examination room and settled into the chair. He popped out for a few minutes, and I knew when he came back, there would be more questions. Not being in the mood to talk, I debated whether I should feign being tired from a lack of sleep and too much excitement, but Dr. Spaulding knew me better than most. I had taught his daughter tumbling, and he'd been my dentist for almost a decade. I was pretty sure he would see through whatever ruse I tried.

When he returned, he took the seat beside me and got right to it: not the dental exam, the questions. "What's going on, Alton?"

"I'm tired and stressed out when I should be happy and content. I've had a lot of things going on in my life, but recently, they've been mostly good."

He asked me what "things" I was referring to. I explained that my book was done and my church family seemed to like it, which was great, but the process of writing the book had caused me to remember things from my childhood I had thought I was done with.

My mom had been dead for a little over a year, and I was still dealing with losing my little sister and her, one right after the other. When I finished, Dr. Spaulding told me he'd recently read an article about the effects of too much stress on a person. The article suggested that it could not only compromise one's health, making a person more prone to fall ill, but it could also cause psychological and emotional issues.

"It's very important, Alton, that you find a way to get rid of some of this stress you're under," he said.

And then he cut to the chase: He said he knew a little about my childhood, and that alone would be reason enough for anyone to seek help from a professional. He explained that most people only see our surface—the smile we wear on our darkest day, the cheery hello we give even if we're crying inside—they fail to see what's going on below.

That can make you think you're fooling the world most days, and maybe you are, but you can't fool your body. What's going on inside you will continue to build, and like a volcano, the stress at some point will become too much for your system to bear, and something will have to give. That's when people explode or drop dead of a heart attack or do something they can't take back.

"I think you may be at that point," said Dr. Spaulding. And he also thought it would be a good idea for me to get some help.

I was in no place to argue with him, and as he finished the exam, I couldn't help but wonder if he knew more about me than I had shared with him. Or was he just that rare observant person who sees beneath the smile?

Before I left the office, I made sure to shake his hand and thank him both for the good advice and for caring enough to say what he had said to me. Back at church, I told Janelda what he had said to me, and she agreed I should go to counseling.

"You should have gone long ago, Alton," she said.

It took a few days for things to settle down and for the weight of what Dr. Spaulding and Kristin had both said to sink in. But when it did, I realized the time to seek help was now.

I needed to do it for myself.

I needed to do it for my kids.

And I needed to do it for Kristin, who had stood by me for so long. For years, I had made half-hearted attempts to be who Kristin said she needed me to be. I now realized the problem was that changing and healing are two different things.

The promise I should have been making to her was the promise to heal. Broken to the point of surrender, I went to see Pastor Mike and asked if he knew of a counselor I could see. He suggested that I go see someone at Stillwater Interfaith Counseling on Pine Street.

*****

Calling Interfaith was the hardest phone call I have ever had to make. I was terrified to make it, and thrilled when no one answered the phone. I did leave my name and number and asked someone to please call me back.

The next morning, a number I didn't recognize came up on my phone, and so I answered it. If I had known who it was, I am sure I would have ignored it.

The call was Susanne Barth returning my call, asking what she could do for me. I explained that I needed to see a counselor and I wanted to get in as soon as possible because I was afraid if I waited too long, I would convince myself yet again that I didn't need help.

The morning of my appointment, I was unsettled, a nervous wreck, and running late for my nine o'clock appointment at Interfaith. I could barely gather my thoughts and struggled finding my car keys; when I finally did, I flew out the door before Kristin had time to wish me good luck.

On the drive over, I made up my mind that I was going to be completely honest from the first session. No matter what was asked of me. No matter how much I did not want to answer. No matter if the answer made me look foolish or weak.

My days of lying to avoid facing the truth or letting the world see the real Alton were over.

For the first time in my life, I not only wanted to be healthy, but I was also willing to do whatever it took to be healthy.

I was committed to revealing what I considered to be the ugly truth of who I was to a total stranger in the hope that it would set me free to be me.

It was as if someone had shot a pistol to start a horse race. Once in Ms. Barth's office, all the things that were eating me inside just poured out.

I shared with her my insecurities about being a father, my issues with my childhood, including my mother's betrayal, neglect, and abuse. I spent the next several Tuesdays telling her the story of my life, the same story I had now written a book about.

"Writing the book caused me to relive a lot of painful moments in my life," I told her. "It's also helped me remember things I had long forgotten or buried, things I thought I had gotten over, but now I'm not so sure."

With each session, it became easier to share the dirt I had hidden from so many people. It felt good being honest with my counselor about everything, and with every secret told, I felt a little bit better.

I had begun to realize that healing was a process, not an end in itself, and it was going to take time to reach a place of peace from which I could look down and see how far I'd come.

Chapter 49

The Plan

After weeks of listening to me and asking what seemed like only a few questions, Ms. Barth told me that she had come up with a treatment plan and goals for me. She handed me a piece of paper and asked me to read it over with her.

"If you have any questions or concerns about anything, you should share them with me," she said, "and we'll discuss them."

At the top of the paper, it read: "Treatment Goals": Alton has written a book revealing his past, and facing that reality has triggered much pain. A goal is attempting to help him acknowledge the past, have a welcoming orientation to difficult and painful emotions, so he will eventually recognize it as his reality and will always be a part of his story.

There followed a page of goals, the first of which I had spent my whole life avoiding: My counselor called it "healing the incest wound."

Just hearing her say the word *incest* almost made me throw up. I sat speechless as she described the signs exhibited by a person who has been a victim of incest. I knew bad things had happened to me as a child, yet I was not ready to accept the words said out loud. I cringed at saying I was a survivor of incest. I had been called all kinds of things in my life, but none of them hurt my heart like that. Ms. Barth could see how much the word pained me, yet she encouraged me to acknowledge it as part of my story. It was a part of who I was, she explained, and unless I faced it head-on, I would continue to struggle.

She used the words *incest wound*, I think, because like a battle wound, it was not of my doing. It had been done to me. I was innocent. I was a survivor. I was not the one who should have been ashamed by what had happened; that was reserved for the person who had committed the crime against me.

It would take me time to realize and accept this.

That first session, I just did my very best not to cry in front of Ms. Barth, although as soon as I was alone in my car, I cried my heart out like I had never cried before.

I felt dirty and like no amount of washing could wash away my newest label. I had heard of incest. I knew what the word meant. Never in a million years, however, would I have used it in reference to myself. I worried that I would not be able to survive the sessions to come without having an emotional breakdown.

The day's session had awakened the shadow that so often turned my dreams into nightmares and kept me awake at night. I was afraid to go to sleep that night, knowing full well that if I closed my eyes, the very reason I was seeing a counselor would return.

My emotions were running so close to the surface that I kept to myself most of the week. I would have skipped youth group, but duty called. When it came time to give my devotion, I found myself talking about how we've all been called names or mean nicknames and how sometimes they can hurt. I told them even though people call us names, God calls us His children, and that should always ring out louder than anything else.

By the time I finished the devotion, I was in tears. I wanted to run and hide but was afraid that would only draw more attention. Through my tears, I saw a room of youngsters looking at me with no evidence of judgment, only pure empathy with what I was going through. Although they didn't know what was bothering me, I could tell that they loved me no matter what it was. I was in a better place by the night's end than when I'd started.

My counselor's second goal for me was to learn how to accept my emotions while remaining fully present. I had always done a very good job of taking the pain from the past and turning it into something else. Ms. Barth was saying that stopped now. She asked me to accept my feelings. Her request didn't make sense to me, and it also scared me. I did not understand how accepting all my emotions was going to do me any good. In fact, I felt I had decided to go to a counselor just so I could move past this very thing. I wanted to get rid of every emotion that left me feeling scared or vulnerable.

Ms. Barth would have none of it. She explained that to heal, I needed to accept how I was feeling. "You have every right to feel hurt because of your past," she said, "but it's not healthy to keep converting those emotions into something else."

The third goal centered on accepting treatment for my anxiety and depression, two problems again that I had ignored in hopes they would just go away on their own.

That meant more than just showing up to my weekly sessions, Ms. Barth said it also meant embracing what was causing me pain and then causing me to hurt others. For her to truly help me, I needed to focus on treatment and how it could change my life.

Her words made sense.

I knew I had issues with depression and anxiety, but I thought I did a good job of hiding it from everyone. When Ms. Barth asked about my symptoms, I told her that when I got depressed, I spent a lot of time in bed, that my depression came and went in spurts, often showing up around Christmastime and my birthday—days that should be special but that instead triggered bad memories.

"I try to fight it off," I said, "but the more I try to fight the dark times, the worse the depression becomes. I cope by just hiding it. I slap on a smile."

The fourth goal I had never heard of before, and it took me a while to understand what Dr. Barth meant by "emotional regulation."

She explained that it meant I had a difficult time letting go of emotions and an even harder time keeping my emotions from consuming me. Instead of accepting what I was feeling, I would transform any confrontation into betrayal; in doing so, I always made things worse than they actually were. I took it personally, so I saw every slight as rejection.

Ms. Barth helped me realize I was far more insecure than I had ever imagined or portrayed myself, and it stemmed from having never been affirmed as a child by anyone in my family—my grandpa being the one exception.

I learned that the reason I hated to disappoint people was because I felt as if my whole life was a mistake, and I could do nothing right. I needed to be right about something in my life; we all do. I had spent my entire life searching for someone, anyone, to be wrong and say they were sorry instead of turning things back on me, when what I really wanted and needed was for specific people to apologize to me for what they had done to me all those years ago. And given that almost all of those people were either dead, jailed, or strung out on drugs, that was not going to happen.

Ms. Barth helped me understand that one reason I respond to emotional matters in an unusual way is because I simply have a hard time identifying the correct emotion.

It's like all of my emotions were put in a bucket and stirred. When it comes time for me to show emotion, I reach in to grab it, but because the emotions have been all mixed up, I might not end up pulling out one well suited for the situation. If I do manage to grab the correct one, it might have another emotion attached.

That meant when I got mad at someone, it was all but impossible for me to be mad without also feeling betrayed. If someone hurt my feelings, I not only felt sadness but I also had a great desire to run.

Learning to regulate my emotions didn't mean I would not feel sadness or happiness. It did not mean that I wouldn't have ups and downs. It simply meant I would learn to accept what I was feeling, allow myself to feel the emotion, and then work to move past it.

My fifth goal had to do with power. On the outside, I appeared tough enough for a guy, and I did my best to hide my issues. Yet as a kid, I had been weak and vulnerable. As an adult, I wanted everyone to think I was as strong or stronger than any other man. That meant adhering to society's expectations that a man should keep his feelings to himself, never show signs of weakness, and never ask for help.

It made me miserable. Ms. Barth helped me to understand that was because it wasn't who I was. I was a man who had been abused and neglected as a child, who sometimes cried at night (and in the day), who struggled with being insecure, who painted flowers, loved babies, and wrote poetry. Yet I was afraid that if people knew all that about me—basically, if they knew me, they would reject me. And that no one would want to be my friend.

I had to learn that real power would give me the strength to accept who and what I was, allowing me to become the man I should be. Real power would eventually give me the courage to admit I could not do what I needed to do by myself.

The sixth issue on the list was shame versus guilt.

I was drenched in both. I was ashamed of myself about the way I had treated Kristin and other people. And because of the incest, I felt that my body also had plenty to be ashamed about. It would take effort to untangle all this.

My seventh goal dealt with boundaries. I had a tendency to get too close to people too fast, and then I'd feel the need to pull away, and to justify that I would look for reasons to dislike them or excuses to push them away.

I have also always had issues with trusting men. That's because most of the men I knew as a boy were neither trustworthy nor particularly good men, and the men who were wealthy and successful made me feel insecure. The latter wasn't the fault of anyone but me. Men who wore suits, drove nice cars, and lived in big houses made me feel less of a man because I had always struggled to pay bills and put food on the table for my family. These men had not done anything wrong to me or mine; I simply wished I had what they had, and my envy caused me to put up walls to keep them at arm's length.

I had also been miserable for so long, and it seemed like wealthy people were always happy. I wanted to be happy and had thought maybe the reason I wasn't was because I was always just getting by.

Aging Out

I know now that being happy isn't about putting up walls and keeping people who are different at a distance. Being happy has nothing to do with where you live or who you hang out with or how much money you have.

If I wanted to be happy, I had to stop pushing people away whose only crime was that they cared about me and I was jealous of them. My sessions helped me realize that true happiness begins with being content. I needed to stop comparing myself to others and be content with what I had; I needed to value what I brought to the table. And I needed to understand the difference between what the TV ads would have us believe constitute riches and what actually makes for a rich life: love, friends, family, a purpose. Those I already had in spades.

Chapter 50

To Be or Not To Be

The fact that I became the father I am should prove that it is possible to become a *good* father—even if you never saw one in your own life. I never saw the men in my life model being a father for me. Nor did I learn how to be a father from my foster parents. And I certainly did not learn how to be a father from my own father.

I never knew my father.

No, I learned how to be a father by watching men do the wrong thing. Although I didn't know what a good father looked like, I was an expert at spotting bad ones—the dads who put themselves first or who put their children in danger, the ones who neglected, shamed, or verbally abused their children. I saw through all of them.

And while I have nothing bad to say about my father's character because I have no idea what kind of man he was or is today, as a child, I wondered about him. Even if he didn't get along with my mom, why didn't he at least claim me? Why did he never come to visit or send a birthday card?

Only a very few times do I remember thinking about how my life might have been different if my dad had stuck around. And those thoughts came and went in a matter of minutes because I had been fatherless my whole life, and I knew no other life.

And there is no room for one now.

The only thing that man could have taught me anyway was how to run away.

More than one person has asked me what I would do if I were to ever meet my father. For years, I didn't have an answer to that question, but now I would say he would only be welcome if he were a stable and good man. I would tell him that I don't expect anything from him and he should expect nothing from me, and that any relationship would be on my terms.

I would keep him away from my wife and children at first, even if he passed muster.

I would demand a DNA test to prove he was my father.

Only with proof in hand would I speak to him.

I would ask him what he has been doing the last forty years, and I would run a background check on him to see what type of life he'd been living and if what he said was true. I would want to know what he did for fun and if he went to church. I would ask if he'd ever been married or had other children. I would do my best not to be judgmental, and I would try my hardest not to ask the one question that would hang in the air: Why did you run out on me?

Instead, I would tell him about me, about my wife and two boys, about the man and father I have become.

I would do my best to set aside my anger over his absence in my life because I have plenty of things in my life to be upset about, and adding one more doesn't seem wise.

All these years later, it would be strange to have my biological father show up and try to start a relationship. And what those years have taught me is not to waste another day hoping for that day to come, if only because I might not like who or what the father who showed up might be.

When I needed him, he wasn't there. Yet I survived. I became the dad I never had, the dad I needed, the dad my sons deserved.

Even though my dad never held me—not once—I knew it was important to hold my two boys. Even though my dad never called me or paid the bills or made sure I had a home or bought me anything for Christmas, I have done all those things for my sons.

Why? Because I knew how bad it hurt me when my father didn't, I chose not to hurt my children in that way. If nothing else, my absent father taught me what not to do, and for that I am grateful.

I might have stumbled around in the dark trying to define myself and figuring out the role of parent and husband, but I did it. I am not perfect, but I am here and present in my wife and sons' lives. I am here because I chose to be different than others in my family. I used the pain that they gave each other and to me as fuel to move forward. In doing so, I swore I would always do all I could to protect my wife and kids from my past, from my family, and from anyone who would try to hurt them.

I made plenty of mistakes—sometimes because I was insecure, sometimes because I didn't know any better—but even though at times I wanted nothing more than to give up, I never did. I am present because I chose to be present. I faced fears of being a parent while doing all I could to heal and conquer my lingering fears.

And one of the reasons I am still here is because I got to see something my father never got to see all those years ago: What the love of a good wife and children feels like.

I learned to be a good dad by watching what not to do.

Sometimes no example might be what's best.

Chapter 51

Quirks

When I finished counseling, I continued to discover things in my life that contained traces of the past. I am striving to put them behind me, but a few still linger from the past and continue to influence my life. Here are some of my quirks that are a direct result of some of my childhood experiences:

Eating in the dark

I can't do it. Growing up with roaches left a lasting impression on me. They crawled across the television, lived in the refrigerator and cabinets, and could be found in the cereal box. Because I grew up with so many bugs, I still cannot eat in the dark as an adult. I will always turn on a light when eating a meal or snack in the kitchen at night for fear of eating a roach. And I always wince when I flip the light switch because as a child, the light always revealed thousands of roaches scurrying for cover.

Only one item on my plate

When eating a meal, I eat one item on my plate at a time because

I'm still always a bit surprised to see more than that. Rarely as a child did I get more than one item of food on my plate, no matter the meal.

Collecting cups

In my childhood, we drank out of mayonnaise jars and pickle jars because we could not afford cups and glasses. I have a tendency to buy cups when we don't need them, and I always keep the plastic cup that comes with a meal from Eskimo Joe's.

Sleeping on the couch

Whenever I am afraid that I might have a bad dream, I refuse to go to bed. Instead, I stay up watching television on the couch. The light of the television makes me feel safe.

Buying socks

My sock and underwear drawers are overflowing, and still I have the urge to buy more. When I was a boy, my socks never matched, and they were always too big. Every time I go to Walmart, not only do I want to buy socks and underwear, but I also stop by the graphic T-shirt section to see if there is a new shirt I might like.

Brushing off compliments

If anyone ever compliments me on the way I look, I am quick to reject it. To this day, I have a hard time understanding why anyone would find me attractive. I still see myself as the split-tooth crybaby whom my uncles and siblings relentlessly teased about his looks.

I share my quirks with you because we all have them. Our personal quirks are one of the things that make us, well, us—and not somebody else. I find that the more I heal, the more I am able to accept not only myself but also my quirks. Although my quirks are traces of the past, they will not decide my future.

There are a few things I would like to undo in my life, but not many. Most of it I would go through again because to change the past would mean to rearrange me, and to rearrange me would mean I was not, well, me.

*****

Like every other person on this planet, I will spend every day for the rest of my life healing and trying my best to become my best self, but I know now that I don't have to do it by myself.

In the past, my attempts at healing were an awful lot like an indecisive person taking a dirty old car to an automatic car wash. I would pull into the bay, and when the presoak started, it would be more than I could handle, and I would try to back out, pulling against the machine designed to pull me through.

There might have been something special up under all of that dirt, but it just hurt too much when the dirt was being washed away.

After counseling, I was able to pull my life into the automatic wash and let it do its job. Going through the car wash hurt more than I could have ever imagined, but now that I am clean, I feel good about who I am. I can accept that I have made terrible mistakes without dwelling on it to the point of self-destruction.

Having been used to being covered in dirt, it made me feel vulnerable to have it washed away. But beneath all that dirt was a man with a bruised heart who deserved love . . . a chance to heal . . . and a second chance.

I have waited more than forty years to be able to say, "I love me."

And I am able to say it now only because there were so many who loved me first, when I could not bear to do so.

Those people loved me in spite of my flaws. And it is because of them that I have learned how to have healthy relationships and to appreciate all that I have survived.

I am a new person because of my faith in God, Kristin, Kelton, Colin, and my church family. I have arrived at a point in my life that I can look at myself in the mirror and not be ashamed of the man I see or who I once was.

Don't get me wrong.

I still have regrets, things I wish I could go back and do over, and I still think about the people I have hurt and let down through the years. But because I have accepted what I have done and what has been done to me, I no longer dwell on the past. I am able to avoid letting such dark thoughts consume me.

I love me.

And the reason why I can now love me is because I have accepted my past. I love the unstable husband struggling to find his place in the world, the husband running scared from his problems, the husband hurting and not willing to heal.

I love me, the man who was angry at the world and did everything he could to self-destruct. I love me, the young man who held onto every hateful thing people said, allowing it to eat at him from the inside out. I love me, the student who left college not once but twice but who proved on the third try that even a learning disability couldn't keep him down. I love me, the boy who survived foster homes and group homes. I love me, the boy who carried bricks and all the abuse he suffered behind a smile. I love me, the boy who was thrown down the stairs and made to feel like he was not part of the family. I love me, the boy who saw his mother get beaten, mistreated, and high on drugs. I love me, the boy whose mother left him home alone and put strange men in front of him and his siblings.

I love me, the boy who was always hungry and who had to have roaches taken out of his ears.

For most of my life, I hated the boy with the gap between his front teeth. I hated the boy who didn't smile for fear that people would make fun of him. I hated the boy who—no matter what he did—could not seem to make his family love him.

Today, that little boy with the gap in his teeth is the screen saver on my computer, a daily reminder of who I was and who I am.

Epilogue

Since the release of my first book, *The Boy Who Carried Bricks*, in 2015, I have been lucky enough to travel all over the United States and share my life story with more than seventy thousand people. I do so with the intent of helping adults and kids who either need to heal or who are in a position to bring healing to someone else.

Sharing the dark parts of my story isn't always easy, but I can keep doing it because in every audience, I see pain in people's faces. If a little hope appears in their eyes before I step off the stage, I've done what I came to do.

Ideally, my message is not about me but about all the people out there experiencing rough times who continue to put one foot in front of the other, who continue to get out of bed each day, who refuse to give up. Those are my people.

After a year, I have had enough conversations with children and adults to know that I am not alone in my struggles . . .

There was the older man in a three-piece suit who approached me after a talk in my hometown. He confided to me he'd also had an awful childhood. "But I would never have the courage to get up and tell people what happened to me," he said. "I would be afraid if people knew what I'd been through that no one would respect me. Thank you for helping me to begin to heal, for letting me know I am not alone." He hugged me and left.

There was the mother who had given my book to her third-grader to read on a family trip. Her daughter read the book the entire trip to California and all the way back. When she finished, she told her mom, "Now I know why Ashley acts the way she does. I bet she has a bad home life like Alton did."

There was the teacher at a small Oklahoma school who burst into tears during in-service training after I told the story of the teacher who kicked me out of class because she couldn't bear to have me around any longer. The woman said she saw herself in that teacher. "I have a lot of respect for you," I said. "It took a lot of courage to say what you just said about yourself." And then I told her if she did see a little of herself in my former teacher, there was still time to change. "A few weeks ago, I received a letter from that fourth-grade teacher," I said. "I was expecting something harsh about what I had written in my book about her. I did not find harsh words at all. What I found was a heartfelt apology for what had happened years ago." All these years later, I told the group, teachers are still making a difference in my life. Reading her letter healed me a little more, and I'd be forever grateful that my fourth-grade teacher took the time to write it.

There was the third-grader at a Tulsa elementary school full of students living in poverty who challenged my story. The school librarian, after hearing me talk to the older students, had suggested I spend some time with the second- and third-graders. I modified my life story a little given their ages, but I let them know I had not only survived a rough childhood but I had also broken the cycle, going on to finish high school and college. When I finished, this third-grader came up and asked, "Is that story really true?" I looked at her and said, "Yes, it is." She said she didn't believe it. "It's my story," I said. "You don't believe what happened to me as a kid? Why?" She looked hard at me: "Because you turned out okay."

And then there were the children at Positive Tomorrows, a school for homeless kids in Oklahoma City, who sat in a circle while I told them about an alcoholic uncle of mine who wasn't very nice to me when I was a little kid. To my surprise, a little boy got up, came over, and whispered in my ear: "My dad is an alcoholic, and he isn't very nice either." Then he returned to his spot in the circle and sat down.

Taken aback a bit, I shared another story, this one about my abusive boys ranch dad. A little boy from the other side of the circle got up, came over, bent down, and whispered in my ear: "My grandpa hits me, too." Then he, too, returned to his place and sat down.

I finished my talk by saying my goal in life is to be a good dad to my two sons. I had no more than said it than the smallest child in the class got up, walked around the circle to me, and whispered in my ear, "I wish you were my dad." I choked back tears as the boy made his way back to his spot in the circle, sat down, crossed his legs, and gave me a big smile.

"I would be proud to have you as a son," I told him.

I left Positive Tomorrows that day knowing some of those very children would sleep in an abandoned building or a car that night. I drove home wishing there was more I could do for them. Nothing I had said to them would change their present living conditions or the behavior of the adults in their lives. The best possible outcome of my visit was that they now knew someone just like them who had made it—and maybe, just maybe, that would give them the hope to do the same. And because a little boy had told me he wished I could be his father, I got a chance to heal a little as well.

*****

In the end, if I could tell any child or adult who has suffered in life one thing, I would say this, "We are survivors."

We have survived what most could not.

And we can take our pain, join together, and help others heal.

As the American author Edward Everett Hale would have us remember: "I am only one, but I am one. I cannot do everything, but I can do something. I will not let what I cannot do interfere with what I can do."

About the Author

A former foster child and police officer, Alton Carter is director of youth ministries for the First United Methodist Church of Stillwater, Oklahoma, and a graduate of Oklahoma State University. He is author of the award-winning books *The Boy Who Carried Bricks* and *Aging Out*. He writes and makes his home in Stillwater. Visit him at www.AltonCarter.net.

I Wish I Had Known

Looking back, there are many things I wish someone would have discussed with me about aging out of the foster care system before I actually aged out, things that could have made a big difference in those first few difficult years on my own.

I share a few here.

I would be completely on my own

I wish someone had told me that once I turned eighteen years old, I would not have anyone checking on me or making sure I was okay. I knew aging out of the system would give me some independence; however, I had no idea I would be completely and utterly on my own—that I would have no safety net whatsoever.

The importance of having a Plan B

I wish someone had explained the need for me to develop not one but two plans for when I aged out of the system—before I actually aged out. Having a Plan B would have meant there was another option for me if Plan A fell apart.

Whom do I call when I need someone

I wish someone had given me a list of names of people or agencies or services to call when I needed help after aging out. When I turned eighteen, I felt all alone, and I lacked a support system to ensure that I did not self-destruct. I had no idea whom to talk to about how to open a checking account, where to go for food if I was hungry but without money, or how to find work. I would have been grateful to have someone to call when in trouble or in need of help or advice.

Once I turned eighteen, my records would be sealed

I wish someone had told me that once I turned eighteen, my court records were sealed. I thought anybody who wanted to find out about my childhood could gain access to my court records. I often thought people knew about me and what I had been through when in fact they hadn't a clue.

What I might expect from my biological family

I wish someone had told me that my family might not welcome me back with open arms. One of my biggest fears was what sort of treatment I would get from my family after I graduated from high school. I had no idea what they expected from me and what I was obligated to do for them now that I was an adult. I wish someone could have explain to me that having not been around them for years would make me feel more than ever like an outsider. And I definitely needed to hear someone say that if I found success, my family might do all they could to take what I earned or to criticize me for not do-ing more for them. It would have been nice to have been forewarned that they might continue to make me feel guilty for having left them for a better life.

That it is okay to go to counseling

I wish someone had told me that it was okay to go a counselor or therapist and talk about what I'd gone through in my childhood; I wish someone had told me about the good that could come from counseling. I had seen many counselors over the years as a foster kid, but not once did I open up and share what was bothering me—the tongue-lashing my mother gave me the one time my brother and I told someone about what had happened in our house still echoed in my head. I wish someone would have told me it was okay to share the things that caused me the most pain. As I got older, I still resisted seeking professional help because I had never seen any adult go to counseling, so I assumed doing so meant you were weak. If I had known that one of the ways for me to heal would be to talk to a counselor and receive professional advice, maybe I would have decided to go and seek help earlier, and that would have been better for me, for my wife, and for our boys.

That I have a choice

I wish someone had told me that no matter what happens in life, I get to choose how to respond. I was constantly fighting my past, and many times, I chose to embrace pain because I thought that was my only option. I wish someone could have explained to me over and over that I had power to choose and that the choice was mine alone. I felt guilty for leaving my family and at times felt like I had no choice but to go back to them at some point. I needed to hear that whatever I chose to do was completely up to me, and I would either reap the benefits or suffer the consequences of my actions. I should have been told over and over again that if I failed in life, it was because I chose to fail, and if I succeeded, it was because I chose to succeed.

What it means to "age out"

Someone should have explained to me that aging out of the system was real and a part of every foster kid's life, and we can survive it.